DECIDE: STUDENT MANUAL

Thomas F. Pray
Rochester Institute of Technology

Daniel R. Strang
State University of New York
College at Geneseo

Random House
Business Division
New York

Preface

We have observed that students enrolled in our management courses gained a "systems viewpoint" to the management process and to the process of business decision making when they participated in a computerized management simulation. We have also found, however, that the simulations on the market were inadequate in many substantive areas. These inadequacies led us to develop our own simulation.

The computerized Management and Economics Simulation, which we have named DECIDE (Decision Exercises through Computer/Instructor Designed Environment), is intended to augment the students' learning in business or management courses. It is particularly well suited for introductory courses in which the students may not be familiar with the principles of management, accounting, finance, and yet experience indicates, it is robust enough to be used as a capstone course for upper-division management/business students.

SIMULATION ENVIRONMENT

We have found from our experience that the most effective implementation of DECIDE occurs when we divide the class into a number of small teams (consisting of three to six people). Each team represents the upper-level managers of a hypothetical company. It is their responsibility to make the appropriate management decisions in a simulated competitive business environment. Each team makes decisions on variables such as price, promotion, production, investment, R & D expenditures, etc. The company's decisions, along with the competitor's decisions, are then "fed" into the computer. The computer program simulates the industry operations and generates operations and financial reports. These reports form the basis for future decisions.

PURPOSE

The simulation (i) introduces the students to dynamics of "real world" management decision making, (ii) provides an opportunity for the students and the instructor to exchange ideas and philosophies on relevant Management and Economic topics, (iii) allows the students to investigate various Management and Economic strategies where the "gains and rewards" are not measured in real dollars but in knowledge acquired, (iv) illustrates the difficulties of management decision making when confronted with "real world problems" such as simultaneous inflation and recession, and (v) places emphasis on viewing all the operations of the firm from a systems standpoint.

COMPUTER SKILLS

The administrator of the simulation need not have computer training. The instructor's manual describes in a "step by step" fashion how the decisions are to be converted into computer cards and how they are to be arranged to run the program.

Even though it is easy to implement the program and the computer runs that follow, the administrator still maintains complete flexibility. For instance, the administrator has the capability to control various parameters such as rates of inflation, recession or boom indexes, and the number of decision variables that the students make, etc. The control cards which are clearly described in the instructor's manual permit the administrator to stress a particular concept or principle without modifying the basic computer program.

DECISION HIGHLIGHTS

We tell the students that the product they are producing and retailing is shoes and that there are two major inputs used in the production process — leather and rubber. (To suit the needs of other institutions, product and input names can be easily changed.)

Each team is required to make approximately thirteen decisions per period (each period represents three months). Some of the major decisions are briefly described below:

Price — The shoes sell for about $25.00 per pair. (At the beginning of the simulation the price elasticity of demand for each team is approximately -3.1, but it can become inelastic through planned promotion and R & D expenditures.) See Appendix #II.

Promotion — At the start of the simulation each team spends approximately $500,000 for promotion. Promotion influences an individual team's share of the market and the total market demand. It is subject to diminishing returns.

Research and Development (R & D) — As in the case of promotion, R & D influences both firm and total market demand. (It also affects the firm's waste factor which is described below.) At the beginning of the simulation, each team spends approximately $300,000 on R & D. (Both previous promotion and R & D expenditures are weighted in the simulation via exponential smoothing techniques.)

Preventative Maintenance — (Maintenance) — Maintenance expenditures influence the smoothness of the production operation. Planned preventative maintenance expenditure (correlated to production levels) will reduce the operating costs via reduction in breakdowns, workstoppages, shortages, etc. (These latter factors are described below under the heading of downtime.) Starting values for maintenance expenditure are about $350,000 per period.

Labor Scheduled — Each team decides on the number of labor hours required to meet their production level. Used and unused labor hours are charged at a rate of $8.00 per hour in the absence of inflation. Overtime labor rates are 1.5 times the regular labor rate. The computer program automatically constrains the hours available for production to the plant capacity.

Raw Materials Purchased — Leather and rubber are the two raw materials which are required to produce one unit of the product (i.e. shoes). Each team must order these raw materials one period in advance. Each pair of shoes produced requires 2.0 square feet of leather and 1.0 square foot of rubber exclusive of waste. Initially, each team should expect about 10% waste for both raw materials. The waste

factor, which is inherent in any production process, can
be reduced through R & D expenditures and some "luck."
(The luck factor relates to R & D breakthroughs and is
simulated by a random number generator contained in the
program.)

Production — Each team must project its sales and plan
its production accordingly. Unsold products are shown
in their finished goods inventory. Production is
automatically constrained if the team does not have
sufficient capacity or raw materials. If the team
stocks out, up to 50% of the stockouts will return
in the next period. (This is determined by the random
"luck" factor.) The remainder of the stockouts return
to the industry and the normal forces of "supply and
demand" determine their allocation. Actual production
level is influenced by a downtime factor.

Downtime — Downtime relates to workstoppages, shortages,
breakdowns, etc. Initially, downtime is about 10% (i.e. 90%
of effective productive time) but can be reduced by an
adequate maintenance policy and by a well planned capital
expenditure program. If the company fails to maintain
and replace the depreciated equipment, downtime will
significantly increase. In addition, if the company
expands (i.e. through capital investment) too rapidly,
downtime could rise to a level of 30 to 50 percent for
the period.

Dividends Paid — In DECIDE, dividend policy is not treated

as a residual decision as in other simulations. Each team's ranking, measured by the stock market value, is heavily influenced by its dividend policy (to be described below). For an optimal dividend policy, teams should correlate their dividends with projected profits. They must also keep a "close eye" on their debt, for too much debt will cause their stock market value to fall.

Securities Bought or Sold — The teams have the option of investing their idle cash into a security market. In this market teams are allowed to buy or sell securities in any amount. Interest is earned on the securities at the rate of 6% annually. If the team chooses to buy securities but fails to provide sufficient cash, the computer program automatically loans them the money at a rate of interest greater than 6%. (With a nominal amount of debt, the interest rate is about 10% annually. However, the rate increases exponentially with the total liability.)

Purchasing Economic Forecasts — Teams have the option of buying economic information specific to their industry. They may purchase information on any or all of the following: seasonal influences of demand for their industry, indexes for the entire economy, and the expected rate of inflation. The forecasts are for 4 periods and relevant costs are illustrated on the computer printout.

Market Information — Teams may also purchase information about their competitors. This information may be aggregate (i.e. averages for the industry) or may be specific to each firm. (They may purchase the following information for all firms in the industry: price, promotion, production, R & D expenditures, and sales).

UNIQUE AND DIFFERENTIATING ASPECTS OF DECIDE

The simulation has the following distinctive features which are not found in many simulations on the market.

(A) Override Option — A unique feature of the simulation is that the administrator can specify the amounts/levels for as many decisions as he wants. This feature permits the instructor to gradually lead into the decision making process. For instance, initially it may be advantageous to restrict team decision making to a few decisions, and then gradually increase the number as the students gain familiarity with the simulation. With this option, the administrator can focus on any one particular area or decision. This permits students to investigate Management and Economic concepts, such as the nature and components of demand elasticities, breakeven analysis, and the importance of sensitivity analysis. It may also be used to minimize the dysfunctional frustration associated with simulation play.

(B) Detailed Financial and Production Worksheets — "Step by step" detailed financial and production worksheets help lead the students through the major decisions. They are particularly helpful in illustrating the

importance and the relative simplicity of cash flow
analysis and profit projections.

(C) <u>Learning by Doing</u> — An advantage of DECIDE over other
simulations is in the stock market function. Not only
does it give proper weight and attention to the dividends,
discounted rate of return on equity and to the debt-equity
ratio, but it also does *not* severely penalize students
for making poor decisions early in the simulation. Thus,
the students can falter early in the game but through
improved decision making can still have a high and
successful stock market rating at the end of the simulation
play.

(D) <u>Administrator's Summary</u> — A convenient summary report
is printed at the end of each computer run. It contains
the major decisions and summarizes each firm's position.
We have found this report to be invaluable for effective
classroom feedback and discussion. It permits the
instructor to (i) react quickly to all team decisions
and the results of those decisions from a single sheet
and (ii) to keep a convenient record of performance over
time. This feature is crucial when the instructor employs
the simulation in large introductory management courses.

(E) <u>Uncertainty</u> — Uncertainty is formally introduced into
the simulation via a self-contained random number generator.
This generator produces a rectangular probability distribution.
The distribution influences (i) R & D breakthroughs which
reduce the waste factor, (ii) breakthroughs of equipment

and workstoppages, either due to inadequate capital formation or overzealous capital expansion, and (iii) the number of returning stockouts to a particular firm. It also introduces noise into the forecast.

(F) <u>Production and Materials Management versus Marketing Emphasis</u> — Other management simulations on the market overemphasize the marketing function. It is our feeling that we have obtained the proper mix by emphasizing the production factors of (i) waste, (ii) downtime, (iii) maintenance, and (iv) R & D along with marketing factors such as (i) promotion and (ii) market and economic research information.

In addition, the finance decisions play a larger role in DECIDE. Dividends, Investment, and Security Management heavily influence the performance and the standing of individual teams.

(G) <u>History</u> — All relevant history needed for computer runs in subsequent periods are punched on computer cards at the end of each computer run. (Three history cards a team are punched.) Thus, no computer tape or disk files are required for the history.

(H) <u>Firm's Demand Function</u> — The firm's demand function is based on its relative exponentially weighted expenditures for R & D, price and promotion. The parameter values and smoothing coefficients used cause the demand to be initially price elastic (i.e. market is extremely responsive to price fluctuations) but through "planned and "realistic" expenditures for promotion and R & D individual demand curves become more inelastic.

(I) <u>Industry Demand Function</u> — The underlying demand function is based on economic theory. We have chosen a multiplicative homogeneous industry demand function where the major independent variables are exponentially smoothed industry average price, promotion and R & D. The initial elasticities for price, promotion, and R & D are -.9, .1, and .05 respectively.

(J) <u>Computer Facility Requirements</u> — The program and its subroutines are written in ANSI (American National Standards Institute) FORTRAN with numerous comment statements to assist the user. It has been tested on various computers (i.e. CDC 6400, Burroughs 4700, IBM 370, DEC 10, XEROX Sigma 9, and Cyber 173). The program and subroutines require approximately 8000 60-bit words of storage on the Cyber 173 and, therefore, will "fit" on all modern computer facilities.

Because the cost of running computer programs varies widely from system to system, it is impossible to state the exact cost of running DECIDE. (However, on the Cyber 173, the C.P.U. time is 1.62 seconds and "our" costs are approximately 12.5 cents per computer run.)

ACKNOWLEDGEMENTS

The authors are grateful to many individuals who have aided them in the development of the simulation and preparation of this text. The authors would like to express their appreciation to the members of the Economics and Management Science Department at the State University of New York at Geneseo for their support, advice, and encouragement. In particular, the authors would like to thank Professors David A. Martin and Michael Crino.

The authors wish to express their appreciation to the personnel in the computer center at SUNY Geneseo for their assistance in the computer program development. The assistance of Walter Robards, Data Center Manager, was especially valuable.

The authors are thankful to Lloyd M. Couvillion, Kenneth Deutsch, and Joseph O'Brien for the time and effort they spent editing and proofreading the manuscript.

A special note of appreciation is given to Professor Richard Butler, of Rochester Institute of Technology, for the many ideas that he provided during the conceptual development stage, and for his support vis-à-vis use of the simulation in his Business Policy classes during the testing stage of development.

We wish to acknowledge the assistance of Theresa McDonald, our student and colleague, for her assistance in manuscript preparation and parameter sensitivity analysis.

Finally, the authors would like to thank the students at SUNY Geneseo and Rochester Institute of Technology who used the simulation. It was their input during the development stages that permitted the authors to "fine-tune" and improve the simulation.

Table of Contents

TABLE OF CONTENTS — CONT.

Chapter One:
DECIDE: An Overview

INTRODUCTION

This chapter of DECIDE briefly describes: (1) the nature of DECIDE, (2) the goals and purposes of the simulation, (3) the requisite skills of the participants, (4) the simulation environment, (5) the team's objectives, (6) the major decisions, (7) the starting values for all teams, and (8) the summary reports. In the chapters that follow the major topics are described in more detail.

WHAT IS DECIDE?

DECIDE is a computerized business simulation designed to assist students in understanding the dynamics of the management decision making process. Just as students of biology, chemistry, and physics have experimental laboratories in which they make their own discoveries that reinforce their classroom lectures, DECIDE permits the students of management and economics to experiment, discover, and reinforce their classroom learning.

BACKGROUND, ENVIRONMENT AND THE OBJECTIVES OF DECIDE

DECIDE was first implemented at the State University College of New York at Geneseo in the Introduction to Management course. The simulation not only assisted the students in learning and understanding fundamental topics

1

of management, economics, accounting, finance, etc., but
allowed them to see the interdependence of each of the areas.
The authors have found that traditional courses in management
and business have a tendency to move from topic to topic in
a fragmented fashion and fail to illustrate the interdependence
of the related topics. The students who participated in
DECIDE, however, acquired a realization of the importance
of an integrated approach to management decision making.

DECIDE illustrates the need for recognizing this
interdependence of decisions in a fashion that the students
find stimulating and enjoyable. Students quickly learn the
importance of viewing decision making from a "systems viewpoint"
and this learning is reinforced by their experience.

DECIDE allows the students to investigate the various
strategies of managing a hypothetical firm in a simulated
business environment. This is accomplished by dividing the
class into small groups or teams. Each team represents the
upper level managers for a firm that manufactures and retails
a single product. This product being produced and sold might
be considered work shoes. In the production of these shoes,
two raw materials are required: rubber and leather. The
teams or the "new" managers assume the role of executive
administrators for an ongoing, successful firm.

Typically, the number of competing firms in the industry
varies between two and nine. An industry with such a limited
number of firms is referred to as an oligopoly. Some
contemporary examples of oligopolies include steel producers,

the aluminum industry, the automotive industry and producers of electronic components. As the participants will discover, the existence of the oligopoly environment will influence the activities and behavior of the firms. Because of the oligopoly structure, the major management decisions that the teams make will *not* go unnoticed by their competitors. Thus, DECIDE introduces students to the challenge of effective management decision making when confronted with the uncertainties of the actions of their competitors.

The managers are subjected to additional uncertainties due to uncontrollable events in the operation of their firm. Even if all teams in the industry made identical decisions, their results would not be the same. As in the real world, DECIDE's uncertainty influences the reliability of forecasts and the efficiency of implementing the factors of production. The managers who are ultimately successful in DECIDE must effectively cope with this uncertainty.

Real world managers must sometimes make difficult decisions when faced with limited funds. Some examples might be: (1) whether to change the emphasis of their operations in one direction or another; (ii) whether to place additional funds in advertising or into quality control; (iii) whether to increase the size or frequency of orders for raw materials. Such real world decisions often involve trade-offs. Careful analysis of these trade-offs is needed to arrive at the best decision. In DECIDE effective management requires the analysis of such trade-offs.

DECIDE allows the students to investigate various strategies of managing their company. Undoubtedly, firms following some strategies will prosper while other strategies will fail and the company involved may falter. What is important, however, is what the students gain from the experience. The real "gains and rewards" from DECIDE are not measured in dollars nor financial-type statements but rather in knowledge acquired by the student participants.

REQUISITE SKILLS

While DECIDE employs the technology of the electronic computer, the participants need not have any prior knowledge of computers or computer programming.

New students of business and management need not have any formal training in the above areas. In fact, DECIDE has been used effectively in classes (both large and small) where the background of the students is extremely diverse.

The authors have found that students without formal training in areas of accounting, finance and/or economics may feel "overwhelmed" during the first few sessions of DECIDE. This is to be expected. It is important that they do not become discouraged, for it normally takes two to three periods to become acquainted with the decision making process of DECIDE.

Students with previous management business training can significantly augment their learning by testing out the theories, strategies, and management philosophies which they have already acquired.

THE SIMULATION PROCESS

During allotted time (either within the class or outside) the team members are required to make approximately thirteen major management decisions. These decisions are then transferred to computer cards. The administrator arranges the cards and inputs them into the computer. The DECIDE program will then simulate the industry and print out financial and operational statements for each firm. These statements are similar to those that stockholders, operating and plant managers, and corporate executives might use in the real world. They are helpful to all parties because they summarize the effectiveness of the decisions made and provide a basis for furture decisions.

Each simulation period represents three months (a fiscal quarter). The simulation is designed to be used for any number of periods up to twenty. At the beginning of the simulation all teams start from the same position. Each team has the same amount of assets (i.e. cash, inventory, plant and equipment, etc.) and the same production capabilities.

As will be described in Chapter 2, there are many different strategies and philosophies that students may undertake in DECIDE. However, each team will be ranked relative to its competitors by a stock market value. Thus, each team has inherently the same objective — to maximize the value of its stock.

THE TEAM'S OBJECTIVE — THE STOCK MARKET FUNCTION

In the corporate world one measure of the well-being of companies is the value of the stock. Similarly, in DECIDE

the company's well-being and the effectiveness of its team's
decisions are gauged by a stock market value. This stock market
"function" is a cumulative measure of each team's profitability,
consistency and effectiveness of the dividend policy, and the
ability to maintain a reasonable amount of debt (liability).
It is imperative that each team gain an understanding of the
impact of its operations and decisions on the major components
of the stock market function. Effective decision making
increases the stock market value.

There are subsidiary goals and objectives that teams might
pursue. Such objectives include achieving the largest share
of the market, the best inventory control policy, and the lowest
cost of production. These subsidiary objectives are left to
the discretion of the individual teams. It is important, however,
to view the operations of the company and the entire decision
making process from the point of view of the total system. No
one subsidiary objective should dominate the primary objective
of the company which is to maintain its viability and increase
its worth as measured by its stock market value.

THE DECISIONS AND STARTING VALUES

As noted earlier, each team is responsible for making
approximately thirteen decisions which are as follows:

Decision Variable	Decision Units
1. Price	dollars
2. Promotion	dollars
3. R & D	dollars
4. Market Research	dollars*
5. Economic Research	dollars*
6. Production Scheduled	units
7. Labor Scheduled	hours
8. Maintenance	dollars
9. Leather Ordered	square feet
10. Rubber Ordered	square feet
11. Capital Investment	dollars
12. Dividends	dollars
13. Marketable Securities	dollars

After the decisions are made, turned in to the instructor and the computer run is completed, the following operations and financial statements are printed out and distributed to each team:

1. Income Statement
2. Cash Flow Statement
3. Balance Sheet
4. Sales Summary
5. Materials Management Report
6. Labor Availability and Utilization Report

---

*Actually, these decisions are yes or no decisions, but a yes indicates that a fixed sum of money has been spent for research.

7. Economic Forecasts

8. Market Research Information

Examples of the operations and financial statements with beginning values for all teams are displayed on Table 1-1 (page 10). This table contains the results for period 0 (the last period of operation of the previous management). The values contained in period 0 are to be used as the basis for the student participant's first decisions.

In the Chapter 2 "Decisions and the Decision Process", and the Chapter 3 "Sample Decisions and Critical Analysis", each of the decisions and the operations and financial statements are described and analyzed in detail.

SUMMARY

DECIDE is a computerized management decision making game. It is intended to augment students' learning of principles of management, accounting, marketing, finance, etc. The simulation exposes the student to the need for viewing management decision making from a systems point of view. DECIDE is particularly suited to new students of management and business and is also flexible and challenging enough to be used by upper-division students.

Student teams will (by making approximately thirteen decisions) simulate the operations and management of a hypothetical company. Each team's overall objective is to maximaze its stock market value. In this oligopoly, maximization of the stock market value requires maintenance of a profitable operation and thorough analysis of dividend and liability policies.

TERMS AND CONCEPTS

computer simulation	oligopoly
systems approach	the thirteen decisions
interdependence	the eight financial and operations statements
uncertainty in DECIDE	period 0, starting values
overall strategy	the fiscal period
trade-offs	

REVIEW AND DISCUSSION QUESTIONS

1. What is the inherent purpose of DECIDE?

2. In the real world there is uncertainty in the management decision making process. In DECIDE, how is uncertainty introduced?

3. Critically comment on the method of evaluation of performance in DECIDE. *STOCK MARKET VALUE*

4. List the thirteen decisions to be made each quarter. How many units of production (i.e. pairs of shoes) were made in period 0?

10

INDUSTRY NO. 5
INCOME STATEMENT FOR PERIOD 0 FOR FIRM NO. 3

MARKETING →

TOTAL SALES REVENUE (388720. UNITS AT 25.00 PER UNIT) PRICE			9718010.
COST OF GOODS PRODUCED:			
BEGINNING INVENTORY FINISHED GOODS	106132.		
LABOR (8.00 PER HOUR)	3146664.		
OVERTIME PREMIUM	560004.		
LEATHER USED (1.50 PER SQ. FT.)	1301853.		
RUBBER USED (2.00 PER SQ. FT.)	867902.		
COST OF GOODS AVAILABLE		5982556.	
LESS: ENDING INVENTORY FINISHED GOODS		130000.	
COST OF GOODS PRODUCED			5852556.
GROSS PROFIT			3865454.
OPERATING EXPENSES:			
SUPERVISORY	341765.		
MAINTENANCE MAINTENANCE	350000.		
DEPRECIATION	415000.		
INTEREST EXPENSES	0.		
ORDERING COST FOR LEATHER	100000.		
ORDERING COST FOR RUBBER	100000.		
CARRYING COST FOR LEATHER	135060.		
CARRYING COST FOR RUBBER	99990.		
CARRYING COST FOR FINISHED GOODS	10613.		
PROMOTION	500000.		
R & D RESEARCH AND DEVELOPMENT	300000.		
MARKET RESEARCH	0.		
ECONOMIC RESEARCH	0.		
MISC. OPERATING EXPENSES	97647.		
TOTAL OPERATING EXPENSES			2450075.
NET INCOME FROM SALES			1415379.
NET INCOME FROM MARKETABLE SECURITIES			7800.
TOTAL TAXABLE INCOME			1423179.
INCOME TAXES			683126.
NET INCOME AFTER TAXES			740053.

MARKETING → PROMOTION

NET PROFIT

TABLE 1-1

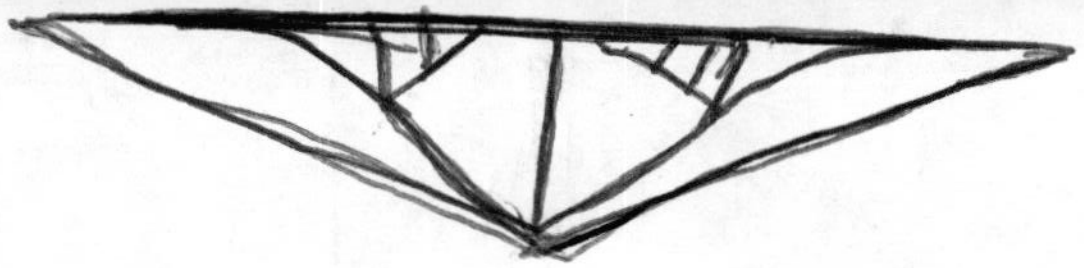

CASH FLOW STATEMENT FOR PERIOD 0 FOR FIRM NO. 3 **MARKETABLE SECURITIES**

CASH INFLOWS:

SALES REVENUE	9718010.
SALE OF MARKETABLE SECURITIES	0.
INTEREST FROM MARKETABLE SECURITIES	7800.
NET INCOME TAX CREDIT	0.
TOTAL CASH INFLOWS	9725810.

CASH OUTFLOWS:

PRODUCTION →RAW MATERIALS PURCHASED PURCHASE OF LEATHER	1301250.
PURCHASE OF RUBBER	868000.
OPERATING EXPENSES REPRESENTING CASH FLOWS	574743.
PURCHASE OF MARKETABLE SECURITIES	0.
DIVIDENDS → DIVIDENDS	70000.
NET INCOME TAX EXPENSE	683126.
FINANCE →INVESTMENT CAPITAL INVESTMENT	815000.
TOTAL CASH OUTFLOWS	9479119.
NET CASH FLOW	246691.

(handwritten) 2*60075.00*
(handwritten) 1,940,680.00

INDUSTRY NO. 5
BALANCE SHEET FOR END OF PERIOD 0 FOR FIRM NO. 3

LIABILITIES:

TOTAL LIABILITIES	0.

EQUITY:

BEGINNING EQUITY	22329947.
ADD: NET INCOME	740053.
LESS: DIVIDENDS	70000.
ENDING EQUITY	23000000.
TOTAL LIABILITY + EQUITY	23000000.

ASSETS:

CASH	3000000.
MARKETABLE SECURITIES	520000.

ENDING INVENTORY:

LEATHER	1350000.
RUBBER	1000000.
FINISHED GOODS	130000.
PLANT BOOK VALUE	17000000.
TOTAL ASSETS	23000000.

(handwritten notes)

Table 1-1

Quarterly Depreciation

PBV X .025 = Min Cap Inv.
or Dept.

PBV X .025 = Depr. or
minimum
capital
⁰Investment

17000000
X .025
425000

2425000

SALES SUMMARY FOR PERIOD 0 FOR FIRM NO. 3

	UNITS	DOLLARS
POTENTIAL SALES	388720.	9718010.
ACTUAL SALES	388720.	9718010.
STOCKOUTS	0.	0.
SHARE OF MARKET 25.0 PERCENT		

MATERIALS MANAGEMENT REPORT FOR PERIOD 0 FOR FIRM NO. 3

LEATHER:	SQ. FT.	RUBBER:	SQ. FT.
BEGINNING INVENTORY	900402.	BEGINNING INVENTORY	499951.
PURCHASED	567500.	PURCHASED	434000.
USED INCLUDING WASTE	867902.	USED INCLUDING WASTE	433951.
ENDING INVENTORY	900000.	ENDING INVENTORY	500000.

WASTE FACTOR 10.0 PERCENT   WASTE FACTOR 10.0 PERCENT

FINISHED GOODS:	UNITS
BEGINNING INVENTORY	8164.
PRODUCED	390556.	**PRODUCTION**
SOLD	388720.
ENDING INVENTORY	10000.	← LEFT IN STOCK

LABOR AVAILABILITY AND UTILIZATION REPORT FOR PERIOD 0 FOR FIRM NO. 3

	WITHOUT OVERTIME	WITH OVERTIME
MAXIMUM LABOR HRS. WHICH COULD BE SCHEDULED FOR PERIOD 0	393333.	590000.
ADD: INCREASE DUE TO CAPITAL INVESTMENT	13583.	20375.
LESS: DECREASE DUE TO DEPRECIATION	6917.	10375.
MAXIMUM LABOR HRS. WHICH CAN BE SCHEDULED FOR PERIOD 1	400000.	600000.

979,400

PRODUCTION ⇒ LABOR SCHEDULED

ACTUAL HOURS SCHEDULED FOR PERIOD 0	440000.
LESS: DOWNTIME (11.24 PERCENT)	49444.
EFFECTIVE LABOR HOURS	390556.

TABLE 1-1

ECONOMIC FORECASTS

SEASONAL INDEX:
PERIOD 0
100.

MARKETING —> **ECONOMIC RESEARCH**   INDEX OF THE ECONOMY:
(NONE REQUESTED)   PERIOD 0
                                         100.

INFLATION INDEX:
PERIOD 0
100.

INDUSTRY NO. 5
MARKET RESEARCH INFORMATION

MARKETING —> **MARKET RESEARCH**   STOCK MARKET (NO RESEARCH COST)
(NONE REQUESTED)

FIRM NO.	VALUE	RANK
1	60.00	1
2	60.00	1
3	60.00	1
4	60.00	1

Page 28

TABLE 1-1

Chapter Two:
Decisions and the Decision Process

INTRODUCTION

This chapter describes: (1) the procedural steps of the simulation process, (2) a framework for decision making, and (3) the decisions and their interrelationships.

THE PROCESS

The administrator establishes management teams for each firm within an industry and assigns each a firm number. If there is a need for more than one industry, each industry is given a unique number from 1 to 9. The firms within an industry are in direct competition only with the other teams in that industry. There is no relationship between different industries. It is the responsibility of each management team to make approximately thirteen quarterly decisions starting from the firm's initial position (i.e. period 0 contained in Table 1-1 [page 10 ff.]).

PROCEDURAL STEPS

Each period the following procedural steps should be followed:

1. Each team reviews reports from previous period or periods.

2. Agreement is reached by the firm's management team on the thirteen major decisions.

3. Decisions are recorded on the decision sheet. (The sheet has been set up to facilitate the keypunching of two computer decision cards.)

4. The two decision cards for each firm in the industry are keypunched.

5. The administrator collects these cards from each firm and makes the computer run.

6. The computerized results are returned to the firms and the cycle is ready to begin again.

OVERRIDE OPTION

DECIDE has within it a provision for the administrator to override any one decision or combination of decisions. If the administrator elects to use this option, each firm will be instructed to ignore certain decisions and leave blank the space provided on the decision sheet.

FRAMEWORK FOR DECISION MAKING

Traditional management theory divides the operation of a manufacturing firm into three functional departments: marketing, production, and finance. It is the responsibility of the marketing department to establish sales plans, develop promotional strategies, oversee production improvements, and estimate potential sales. The production department, supplied with information from the marketing department, tailors the production facilities to accommodate projected needs. In addition, the production department provides input into the development of marketing strategies based upon production potential and inventory levels. The finance department is primarily involved with the procurement and consequent planned usage of capital. This orientation is useful in the management of the simulated firms and facilitates the description of the decision variables (see Figure 2-1 below).

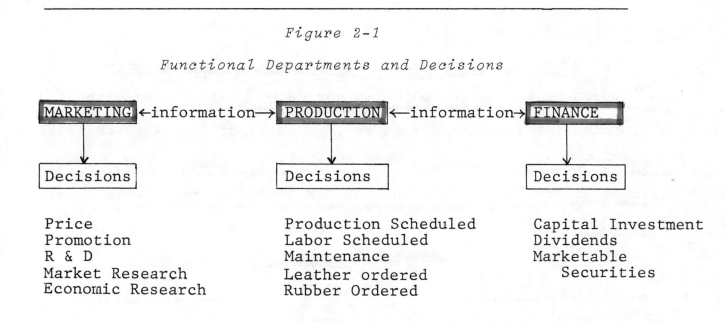

Figure 2-1

Functional Departments and Decisions

| MARKETING | ←information→ | PRODUCTION | ←information→ | FINANCE |

| Decisions | | Decisions | | Decisions |

Price	Production Scheduled	Capital Investment
Promotion	Labor Scheduled	Dividends
R & D	Maintenance	Marketable
Market Research	Leather ordered	Securities
Economic Research	Rubber Ordered	

Although the decisions are conveniently associated with specific departments for the purpose of illustration, the DECIDE manager should be cautioned. For effective management it is imperative that the managers be aware that all decisions are interrelated and, therefore, should not be relegated exclusively to the domain of one department. It is equally important to recognize that the decisions for one period must relate to previous and subsequent periods. Careful planning

18

with a multi-period time horizon is required. The recognition
of the interrelationships described above represents the
foundation of the concept of management called the *Systems
Approach*.* Basically this means that all decisions of
departments must be coordinated to insure successful management.
This is true in the "real world" and will be discovered in
the simulation process.

THE DECISIONS

The decisions involving price, promotion, and research
and development constitute the marketing mix. If a team plans
to pursue a predetermined strategy, it is important that the
three component decisions of the "mix" be coordinated and
balanced over time so that the desired consumer response is
insured.

1. Price — is an important determinant of the sales
   potential of a firm. Specifically, the impact of
   price on a firm's sales potential is determined by
   the firm's price relative to the average industry
   price. It is also dependent on the firm's historical
   pricing pattern. Before expenditures on promotion
   and research and development have changed the
   consumer awareness and acceptance of the firm's
   product through product differentiation, the response
   in sales potential to a firm's price deviation from
   the average will elicit a significant response (i.e.

*For further information on the Systems Approach see *The
Systems Approach* by C. W. Chruchman, Dell Publishing Co., 1968.

a relatively low price will generate a high sales potential and vice versa), but it is possible over time to differentiate the product by well-planned promotion and R & D expenditures. In the real world the philosophy of low price-high volume-lower quality is pursued by some merchandisers known as discounters. The philosophy of high price-low volume-high quality is pursued by merchandisers referred to as specialty shops. Either of these strategies (or some intermediate strategy) can be pursued by the firms in DECIDE. It is left to the participants to discover which strategy is most fruitful. Each firm should establish a price strategy and attempt to maintain it over a period of time. In addition, the successful firm will tailor the quality and production decisions to coincide with this strategy.

The work shoes sold for *$25 per pair* in *period 0.* The average total cost of production and selling expenses was roughly *$16 per pair.*

2. Promotion — Consumers become aware of the availability of the product and its unique features through expenditures on promotion. Included in promotion are advertising on radio and television, store displays, advertisements in newspapers and magazines,

and special promotional campaigns such as games and contests. In DECIDE, the participants need not be concerned with how the funds are allocated to the specific promotional areas. Thus, in DECIDE the promotion decision is an aggregate dollar expenditure.

The impact of promotion on sales potential is determined by the firm's expenditure on promotion (relative to the industry average) and is also dependent on the firm's historical pattern of promotional expenditure. As in the real world, consumers are influenced for a period of time by promotion to which they have been exposed. The level of influence declines with the passage of time. A planned and consistently maintained level of promotional expenditures from period-to-period is likely to be the most beneficial. Expenditures in excess of those required to meet the firm's objectives are not particularly beneficial. The *period 0 expenditure for promotion was $500,000*.

2.3. Research and Development (R & D) — Expenditures in research and development have a twofold effect: (i) they are used to differentiate the product (and, therefore, increase the quality as perceived by consumers) (ii) they are used to minimize the loss (i.e. waste factor) in the conversion of the two raw materials into the finished product.

Significant product improvements and R & D expenditures are essential for the firm which pursues a high quality product. It may require a planned expenditure program for several periods to generate significant product improvements for several periods, but this awareness decreases over time. To maintain a competitive product, nominal expenditures are necessary for those firms not emphasizing high quality.

Expenditures on research and development may also lead to savings through reducing the waste factors. To pursue these savings, expenditures above the industry average are necessary. As in the real world, there are no guarantees of waste reduction break-throughs so the firm must also enjoy some "luck" in order to realize these reductions. The *initial level* of research and development expenditure is *$300,000*.

4. Market Research — It is important in the development of a marketing mix that the firm keep abreast of the activities and expenditures of competitors. Procurement of information concerning competitors does not occur without a cost. Firms can obtain information concerning competitors' marketing mixes (price, promotional expenditures and expenditures on R & D). Firms can obtain values for each firm or the average (mean) for all firms within the industry for any or all of the

marketing mix items. The cost for an *average* for any of the *three items* for a period is *$50,000*. The cost for specific values for *each firm* in the industry is *$100,000* per item.

One measure of the effectiveness of a firm's marketing mix is its sales relative to the sales of competitors. For a *cost* of *$100,000* a firm can determine the specific sales of *each firm* in the industry. The *cost* for the *average* of all firms is *$50,000*.

5. Economic Research — The sales potential of a firm varies in response to the firm's decisions, decisions of its competitors, and external influences beyond the control of firms in the industry. The external influences include changes in the economy and seasonal changes in demand for the specific product. Although the firm cannot control these factors, it is important that it be aware of them.

Information concerning changes in the economy and changes in seasonal demand is typically reported in the form of index numbers based on 100. An increase from the starting level is denoted by a number larger than 100 and a decrease by a number less than 100. The greater the deviation from the index for the previous period, the greater the actual change. The magnitude of the change roughly approximates a percent (i.e. a change in an index from 95 to 100 is roughly equal to a 5% increase).

The seasonal and economic indexes in DECIDE are set initially at *100*. An increase in the economic index is an indication of a general increase in the level of all economic activity for the entire economy and will, therefore, be reflected by an increase in sales potential for all firms. The seasonal index is a measure of consumer buying patterns for the specific industry (i.e. the shoe industry). An increase in this index will, in general, cause an increase in the sales potential for all firms in the industry.

The seasonal and economic indexes are given for each period. Forecasts for the next four periods can be obtained at a *cost: $100,000* for the *seasonal forecasts* and *$75,000* for the *economic forecasts*. The participant should be cautioned that the forecasts are estimates and, therefore, may not be totally reliable. Moreover, the further into the future the projection reaches, the less reliable the forecast is apt to be. Management teams should give careful consideration to the costs and benefits of the information. The information can be purchased every period or less frequently.

Information concerning the general level of prices of the economy (i.e. the inflation index) is also available. The inflation index is reported with a base of *100* and costs the firm *$25,000* for the forecasts for the next four periods. The impact of inflation results in increasing costs of manufacturing and sales. Included in these costs are the cost of labor, raw materials, supervision, miscellaneous expenses and the costs of maintenence of inventories. In the absence of corresponding price increases, inflation will increase a firm's expenses and reduce profits.

All industrial concerns must do at least two things. One is to produce something (i.e. a product or service); the other is to market whatever is produced. Production entails the procurement and utilization of the factors of production which include labor, materials, and plant and equipment. In DECIDE, there are five interrelated production management decisions.

6. Production Scheduled — There are two factors to be considered in scheduling production; (i) the number of units of the finished product needed for anticipated sales and (ii) the production capacity for a given period. The number of goods which can be produced in a given period may be constrained by the availability

of labor or raw materials. For the purpose of the
simulation, *if* the *production scheduled* for a period
exceeds the *number of units which can be produced*
due to constraints, *production* will be automatically
limited to the maximum constrained production level.

7. Labor Scheduled - Each period a decision is made
concerning the number of labor hours to be scheduled.
At the beginning of the simulation labor costs $8.00
per hour for regular time and $12.00 (time and a
half) per hour for overtime. These costs are subject
to change due to inflation. It is assumed that these
costs include all remunerations including fringe
benefits paid by the firm to the workers.

The maximum labor hours which can be scheduled for
a period is reported on a firm's labor availability
report from the most recent period. (Note: the
maximum capacity of a firm can be altered by capital
investment. This is discussed in the latter part
of this section.)

A firm may schedule any number of labor hours up to
the maximum with overtime, but it is charged at the
appropriate rate for all hours scheduled. In the
"real world" each hour scheduled is not always
totally productive. Therefore, in DECIDE, machinery

breakdowns and other workstoppages are to be anticipated and are reported as the downtime percentage. Downtime labor hours must be paid for but are totally unproductive. In most cases the downtime percentage will be approximately 10%, but downtime is dependent on several related decisions to be discussed later. In the *absence* of *downtime*, it requires *one hour of labor to produce one unit* of *finished product*.

In general, each firm should determine its desired production and then schedule sufficient labor hours with an allowance for estimated downtime.

For the finished goods that are not sold, there is a *carrying cost* associated with maintaining and storing the product. The cost is equal to 10% of the value of beginning finished goods inventory and is based on factors associated with finished goods storage such as rental of space, inventory insurance, deterioration, etc.

8 & 9. **Leather Ordered and Rubber Ordered** — Once raw materials are ordered, it requires one period for them to be available for production. It requires *2 sq. ft. of leather* and *1 sq. ft. of rubber, exclusive of waste,* to produce a pair of shoes. Initially, both raw

materials are subject to a *10% waste factor*. Leather and rubber are ordered in units of square feet and *cost $1.50* and *$2.00* per sq. ft., respectively.

Because there is a *carrying cost* associated with maintaining and storing these materials, it is desirable to order only sufficient raw materials to accommodate planned production requirements. This cost is equal to *10%* of the value of the beginning inventory and is based on factors associated with raw materials storage such as rental space, insurance, taxes, deterioration, etc. In addition, the cost of placing an order for either raw materials (independent of size) is *$100,000*.

10. Maintenance — Expenditures for maintenance are needed to insure smoothness of the production process. If insufficient funds are allocated to maintenance, the firm's downtime percentage will increase, and, as a consequence, scheduled labor hours will be wasted.

Maintenance expenditures should be correlated to production levels (i.e. the higher the production scheduled, the larger the expenditures for maintenance). Excess expenditures on maintenance serve no purpose and, therefore, are wasteful. It is left to the management team to experiment and to determine the optimal level of maintenance. The expenditure for *period 0* was *$350,000.*

As described earlier, the third basic function of a manufacturing firm is finance. In DECIDE, as in the real world, the major production and marketing decisions require the utilization of the firm's funds. In DECIDE, the major finance decisions are represented by capital investment, dividend policy, and sale or purchase of marketable securities.

11. Capital Investment — In period 0, the labor capacity is 400,000 hours without the use of overtime and 600,000 hours with full overtime. As machinery wears out due to *depreciation* (which occurs at an *annual rate of 10%*), the capacity will decrease correspondingly. Capital investment is necessary to maintain or increase capacity. A capital investment expenditure equal to the rate of depreciation will just maintain capacity. For each *$60 increment* invested *in excess of the depreciation*, the plant capacity will increase by *one labor hour*. This increase in capacity is subject to depreciation. Either a failure to maintain capacity or an overzealous capital investment program may lead to a machinery breakdown or workstoppages. These, in turn, will cause an increase in the downtime percentage for the period. If significant expansion is planned, it is recommended that the capital invest-

ment program be consistent from period to period.

While overzealous capital expansion programs may

lead to initial increases in the downtime factor,

properly planned capitalization may lead to significant

reduction in downtime.

12. Dividends — The stockholders, the owners of the firm,

have invested money with the expectation of receiving

dividends. Dividend policy is one factor which

influences the firm's stock market value. Previous

managers of the simulated firms in DECIDE have found

that they maximized the effect of dividends on the

stock market by adhering to the following guidelines:

(i) during bad periods the firms have declared dividends

of at least $25,000, (ii) during profitable periods

they have paid dividends equal to 10% of the net

income after taxes. It is recommended that the new

managers estimate the income after taxes and then

decide to declare either the historical minimum or

10% of the estimated income.

13. Marketable Securities — Idle cash reserves maintained

by a firm serve no purpose. Low interest paying (6%

per year) marketable securities can be purchased to

avoid excess cash reserves. In periods in which a

need for additional cash is projected, these securities

can be sold and thereby readily converted into cash.

30

There is no time delay or brokerage costs associated
with these transfers.

ADDITIONAL INFORMATION CONCERNING DECISIONS

It is not expected that the reader has become an expert
in making the DECIDE management decisions based on the preceding
section. If this were the case, there would be no need for the
simulation. Further assistance in understanding the decisions
is provided in the next chapter in which sample period
decisions are analyzed; the learning is extended in Chapter
4 in which the decisions are discussed more technically, and
achieved, finally, through the actual simulation experience.

SUMMARY

The administrator will aid in the formation of the DECIDE
teams. The procedural steps for each period include making
decisions, encoding decision sheets, keypunching, and making
the necessary computer runs.

Effective management decisions require an integrated
approach to the three manufacturing functions: marketing,
production, and finance.

The marketing mix consists of the decisions of price,
promotion and R & D. These three decision variables must be
coordinated because they have a significant influence on
sales and the profitability of each firm.

The production function requires the procurement and
utilization of the factors of production, which include labor,

materials, and capital. There are five interrelated production decisions.

The third basic function is finance. Finance involves procurement and utilization of funds. There are three finance decisions in DECIDE.

TERMS AND CONCEPTS OF THE CHAPTER

procedural steps

functional departments

responsibility of departments
 in DECIDE

marketing mix

systems approach

product differentiation

breakdowns

carrying cost

order cost

depreciation

stockholders

indexes

REVIEW AND DISCUSSION QUESTIONS

1. What three decisions predominantly influence a firm's sales potential?

2. What impact does research and development have upon the waste factor?

3. What is the optimal dividend policy in DECIDE?

4. What information is available concerning competitors? What does it cost?

5. Differentiate between the "three indexes."

6. What are the major constraints imposed upon the production decision for any period?

7. What role does the maintenance decision play in DECIDE?

8. Is it profitable to borrow money and buy marketable securities?

9. Can depreciation expenses ever be advantageous to a firm?

10. Using period 0 results, calculate the investment decision needed to allow the firm to produce 650,000 pairs of work shoes in period 2. (Assume this entails operating at full overtime.)

Chapter Three:
Sample Decisions and Results
for a Hypothetical Firm

INTRODUCTION

This chapter describes the decision making process for a hypothetical firm #3 in a four firm industry. The decisions, results, and analyses that are presented represent those for period 1.

The objectives of this chapter are (i) to provide the reader with additional details concerning the DECIDE decision making process, (ii) to offer guidance in reading and interpreting the financial and operating statements generated each fiscal period, (iii) to illustrate the benefits of *ex post* analysis, and (iv) to emphasize the interrelated nature of the decisions.

STRATEGIES AND DECISIONS OF HYPOTHETICAL FIRM, FIRM #3

It is traditional management theory that one of the most important functions of upper-level managers is planning. Early in the simulation process the participants should develop clear and concise objectives. Based upon these objectives, short, intermediate, and long-term strategies should be formulated.

The management team of firm #3 established a *short-run strategy which called for maximum production, an aggressive marketing mix, immediate acquisition of all research information and a moderate plant expansion.* In the sections to follow, the team's decisions will be described and reviewed in detail.

MARKETING MIX

With this strategy in mind, the managers decided to increase significantly all of the marketing mix factors. They increased their Research and Development expenditures from $300,000 to $800,000, an increase of 167%. In addition, they decided to increase promotion expenditures from $500,000 to $800,000 (a 60% increase). They anticipated that these decisions, in conjunction with a 10% increase in price (from $25 in period 0 to $27.50 in period 1), would allow them to increase both sales potential and revenues. To assist them in future decision periods, they requested the most detailed Economic and Marketing research information available.

PRODUCTION FUNCTION

To formulate their production decisions, the team utilized a special production worksheet. Their sample worksheet is illustrated in Figure 3-1 (page 35). Additional forms are provided at the end of the text. It is recommended that the DECIDE managers utilize these forms in making the production-oriented decisions: desired production, labor scheduled, maintenance, and purchase of raw materials.

DECIDE (PRODUCTION WORKSHEET) FOR TEAM _3_ INDUSTRY _5_ PERIOD _01_

ESTIMATE FOR MAXIMUM PRODUCTION

RAW MATERIAL CONSTRAINTS AND ESTIMATES FOR WASTE AND DOWNTIME   P12

LEATHER: (A) _.10_ = WASTE FACTOR % ÷ 100.   RUBBER: (B) _.10_ = WASTE FACTOR % ÷ 100.   LABOR: (C) _.1124_ = DOWNTIME % ÷ 100.

1. _900,000_ (BEGINNING INVENTORY IN SQ. FT.)   1. _1,500,000_ (BEGINNING INVENTORY IN SQ. FT.)   LABOR CONSTRAINT

Amount of leather wasting

- 2. _90,000_ (1. × (A))   - 2. _50,000_ (1. × (B))   1. _600,000_ (CAPACITY IN LABOR HOURS WITH OVERTIME

3. _810,000_ sq. feet of leather to make   =   - 2. _67,440_ (1. × (C))   _Hours we waste Non-Productive_

= 3R _450,000_ (MAXIMUM PRODUCTION BASED UPON RUBBER CONSTRAINT)   3LA _532,560_ (MAXIMUM PRODUCTION BASED UPON THE LABOR CONSTRAINT)

3L _405,000_ (3. ÷ 2.00: MAXIMUM PRODUCTION BASED UPON LEATHER CONSTRAINT)   _Amount of shoes we can make w/our labor._

DESIRED PRODUCTION _405,000_ 1DP

CHOOSE THE SMALLEST OF (3R, 3L, and 3LA) FOR MAXIMUM PRODUCTION _405,000_ 1MP

ESTIMATE OF RAW MATERIALS USED AND ENDING INVENTORY FOR LEATHER AND RUBBER

LEATHER: RUBBER:

1. _900,000_ (BEGINNING INVENTORY IN SQ. FT.)   1. _1,500,000_ (BEGINNING INVENTORY IN SQ. FT.) Period 0

- 2. _900,000_ (MATERIAL USED: [1DP _405,000_ ÷ [1.00 - (A) _.10_]] × 2.00)   - 2. _450,000_ (MATERIAL USED: [1DP _405,000_ ÷ [1.00 - (B) _.10_]])

+ 3. _900,000_ (RAW MATERIAL PURCHASED IN SQ. FT.)   + 3. _450,000_ (RAW MATERIAL PURCHASED IN SQ. FT.)

= 4. _900,000_ (ENDING INVENTORY IN SQ. FT.)   = 4. _1,500,000_ (ENDING INVENTORY IN SQ. FT.)

ESTIMATE OF LABOR REQUIRED TO MEET DESIRED PRODUCTION (1DP) _405,000_ Pairs of shoes
← # of labor hours needed to produce

1. _456,287_ (LABOR REQUIRED: [1DP _405,000_ ÷ [1.00 - (C) _.1124_]])

Pay more for OT

FROM PREVIOUS PERIOD'S LABOR AVAILABILITY AND UTILIZATION REPORT AND THE ESTIMATE OF LABOR REQUIRED:

TOTAL REGULAR TIME HOURS REQUIRED _400,000_

TOTAL OVERTIME HOURS REQUIRED _56,287_

① Subtract waste factor

```
  1.00
- .10
  .90  450,000
       405,000
```

② Divide answer into desired production

```
    1.0000
 .1124 )1.
```

= Dick's math!

labor

456,387 Amount of hours to produce shoes

```
   456,387
 .8876 )405,405,000
        405,405,000
```

Amount of hours to produce desired production

PRODUCTION WORKSHEET STEPS

The steps in using the special worksheet are as follows:*
(see Figure 3-1 [page 35])

1. Raw Material and Labor Constraints — Insert in the
   spaces provided the Beginning Inventory in square
   feet for the two raw materials and the capacity in
   Labor Hours with *full* overtime. These values can
   be obtained each period from the most recent Materials
   Management and Labor Availability and Utilization
   reports.

2. Waste and Downtime Percentages — The waste percentages
   are subject to both the level of R & D expenditures
   and the occurrence of breakthroughs. In DECIDE, for
   a firm to be considered for waste reduction, its
   pattern of R & D expenditures must be above the industry
   average. (See Chapter 2 — R & D decisions, page 20.)

   Downtime is influenced by maintenance, depreciation,
   capital investment, and production levels. All four
   factors must be evaluated in the estimation process
   for the downtime percentage. (See Chapter 2 —
   Maintenance and Capital Investment, pages 27-28.)

3. Maximum Production (MP) — Following the worksheet,
   calculate an estimate of the maximum production based

---

*The following conventions are used for the production worksheet:
  a) Lines are designated by letters and numbers (e.g. 1DP, 1MP,
     etc.)
  b) Numerical constants are designated by the value and two
     zeros after the decimal (e.g. 2.00, 1.00 and 100.00, etc.)

upon the constraints of rubber, leather, and labor.
(Choose the smallest of 3R, 3L, and 3LA.)

4. Production Schedule — Decide upon desired production
(DP). Desired production may be set (i) below the
estimated maximum production, (ii) equal to it, or
(iii) greater than the maximum. In the third case,
production will automatically be limited by DECIDE
to the maximum possible quantity. (Enter this
decision on line 1DP.)

5. Estimate of Raw Materials Used and Ending Inventory —
Based upon the desired production (1DP), the quantity
of raw materials used (including waste) is estimated.
From this estimate, the managers decided on the
quantity of each raw material that must be purchased
to accommodate the projected production requirements
for the subsequent period(s).

6. Estimate of Labor Required to Meet Desired Production —
Based upon the information above, the total labor
required is estimated (including the downtime loss
and overtime needed). This information is used in
the financial worksheet.

The use of the production worksheet is illustrated for
the hypothetical firm. The period 0 values served as starting
values and are illustrated in Figure 3-2 (pages 38ff.). The
estimates for waste factors and downtime were made by assuming
no change from period 0.

Figure 3-2

INDUSTRY NO. 5

INCOME STATEMENT FOR PERIOD 0 FOR FIRM NO. 3

TOTAL SALES REVENUE (388720. UNITS AT 25.00 PER UNIT)	9718010.
COST OF GOODS PRODUCED:	
BEGINNING INVENTORY FINISHED GOODS	106132.
LABOR (8.00 PER HOUR)	3146664.
OVERTIME PREMIUM	560004.
LEATHER USED (1.50 PER SQ. FT.)	1301853.
RUBBER USED (2.00 PER SQ. FT.)	867902.
COST OF GOODS AVAILABLE	5982556.
LESS: ENDING INVENTORY FINISHED GOODS	130000.
COST OF GOODS PRODUCED:	5852556.
GROSS PROFIT	3865454.
OPERATING EXPENSES:	
SUPERVISORY	341765.
MAINTENANCE	350000.
DEPRECIATION	415000.
INTEREST EXPENSES	0.
ORDERING COST FOR LEATHER	100000.
ORDERING COST FOR RUBBER	100000.
CARRYING COST FOR LEATHER	135060.
CARRYING COST FOR RUBBER	99990.
CARRYING COST FOR FINISHED GOODS	10613.
PROMOTION	500000.
RESEARCH AND DEVELOPMENT	300000.
MARKET RESEARCH	0.
ECONOMIC RESEARCH	0.
MISC. OPERATING EXPENSES	97647.
TOTAL OPERATING EXPENSES	2450075.
NET INCOME FROM SALES	1415379.
NET INCOME FROM MARKETABLE SECURITIES	7800.
TOTAL TAXABLE INCOME	1423179.
INCOME TAXES	683126.
NET INCOME AFTER TAXES	740053.

CASH FLOW STATEMENT FOR PERIOD 0 FOR FIRM NO. 3

CASH INFLOWS:	
SALES REVENUE	9718010.
SALES OF MARKETABLE SECURITIES	0.
INTEREST FROM MARKETABLE SECURITIES	7800.
NET INCOME TAX CREDIT	0.
TOTAL CASH INFLOWS	9725810.
CASH OUTFLOWS:	
PURCHASE OF LEATHER	1301250.
PURCHASE OF RUBBER	868000.
OPERATING EXPENSES REPRESENTING CASH FLOWS	5741743.
PURCHASE OF MARKETABLE SECURITIES	0.
DIVIDENDS	70000.
NET INCOME TAX EXPENSE	683126.
CAPITAL INVESTMENT	815000.
TOTAL CASH OUTFLOWS	9479119.
NET CASH FLOW	246691.

INDUSTRY NO. 5

BALANCE SHEET FOR END OF PERIOD 0 FOR FIRM NO. 3

ASSETS:
CASH	3000000.
MARKETABLE SECURITIES	520000.

ENDING INVENTORY:
LEATHER	1350000.
RUBBER	1000000.
FINISHED GOODS	130000.
PLANT BOOK VALUE	17000000.
TOTAL ASSETS	23000000.

LIABILITIES:
TOTAL LIABILITIES	0.

EQUITY:
BEGINNING EQUITY	22329947.
ADD: NET INCOME	740053.
LESS: DIVIDENDS	70000.
ENDING EQUITY	23000000.
TOTAL LIABILITY + EQUITY	23000000.

SALES SUMMARY FOR PERIOD 0 FOR FIRM NO. 3

	UNITS	DOLLARS
POTENTIAL SALES	388720.	9718010.
ACTUAL SALES	388720.	9718010.
STOCKOUTS	0.	0.

SHARE OF MARKET 25.0 PERCENT

MATERIALS MANAGEMENT REPORT FOR PERIOD 0 FOR FIRM NO. 3

LEATHER:	SQ. FT.
BEGINNING INVENTORY	900402.
PURCHASED	867500.
USED INCLUDING WASTE	867902.
ENDING INVENTORY	900000.

WASTE FACTOR 10.0 PERCENT

RUBBER:	SQ. FT.
BEGINNING INVENTORY	499951.
PURCHASED	434000.
USED INCLUDING WASTE	433951.
ENDING INVENTORY	500000.

WASTE FACTOR 10.0 PERCENT

FINISHED GOODS:	UNITS
BEGINNING INVENTORY	8164.
PRODUCED	390556.
SOLD	388720.
ENDING INVENTORY	10000.

LABOR AVAILABILITY AND UTILIZATION REPORT FOR PERIOD 0 FOR FIRM NO. 3

	WITHOUT OVERTIME	WITH OVERTIME
MAXIMUM LABOR HRS. WHICH COULD BE SCHEDULED FOR PERIOD 0	393333.	590000.
ADD: INCREASE DUE TO CAPITAL INVESTMENT	13583.	20375.
LESS: DECREASE DUE TO DEPRECIATION	6917.	10375.
MAXIMUM LABOR HRS. WHICH CAN BE SCHEDULED FOR PERIOD 1	400000.	600000.

ACTUAL HOURS SCHEDULED FOR PERIOD 0	440000.
LESS: DOWNTIME (11.24 PERCENT)	49444.
EFFECTIVE LABOR HOURS	390556.

ECONOMIC FORECASTS

SEASONAL INDEX:
PERIOD 0
100.

INDEX OF THE ECONOMY:
PERIOD 0
100.

INFLATION INDEX:
PERIOD 0
100.

Using the worksheet, the managers of firm #3 decided to schedule 405,000 units to be produced, ordered 450,000 sq. ft. of rubber, 900,000 sq. ft. of leather, and scheduled 450,000 hours of labor. Note: 450,000 hours of labor were scheduled instead of 456,287 in anticipation of a slight reduction in the downtime percentage. This anticipated reduction was based upon increasing maintenance expenditure from $350,000 to $1,000,000 and by a modest capital investment expenditure.

THE FINANCIAL FUNCTION

A financial worksheet was utilized by the team managers to facilitate making the finance decisions: capital investment, purchase or sales of marketable securities, and dividend policy. Their example worksheet is illustrated in Figure 3-3 (page 41) and additional forms are available at the end of the text.

FINANCIAL WORKSHEET

The financial worksheet can be completed only after tentative marketing and production decisions have been made. In the absence of better criteria, previous period values serve as an estimate for selected items of the estimated income and cash flow statements.**

The most difficult and most crucial estimate to be made is the estimate of sales of the firm for the period. This may require some "heroic" judgment by the managers, yet is essential.

**For further details concerning the accounting aspects of cash flow and income statements see Appendix I, page 91.

DECIDE FINANCIAL WORKSHEET FOR TEAM 3 INDUSTRY 5 PERIOD 01

ESTIMATED INCOME STATEMENT AND CASHFLOW BASED UPON SALES 415,000 1S AND A PRICE OF 27.50 1P

INCOME STATEMENT ESTIMATED:

max # of prs. of shoes they can sell

1. TOTAL SALES REVENUE (1S 415,000 x 27.50 1P) = 11,412,500 1.

Price

		COST OF GOODS PRODUCED:	
		BEGINNING INVENTORY OF FINISHED GOODS =	130,000
a	+	LABOR $8. x 400,000 →	3,200,000
b	+	OVERTIME PREMIUM $12 x 50,000 →	600,000
	+	LEATHER USED	1,350,000
	+	RUBBER USED	900,000
	=	COST OF GOODS AVAILABLE	6,180,000
	-	ENDING INVENTORY OF FINISHED GOODS	0
2.	=	COST OF GOODS PRODUCED	6,180,000 2.
3.	=	(1. - 2.) GROSS PROFIT (1. 11,412,500 - 2. 6,180,000) =	5,232,500 3.

OPERATING EXPENSES: (ESTIMATES)

c	Supervisory	341,765
d	Maintenance	1,000,000
-	Depreciation	415,000
e	Interest Expense	0
f	Ordering Cost for Leather	100,000
g	Ordering Cost for Rubber	100,000
h	Carrying Cost for Leather	135,000
i	Carrying Cost for Rubber	100,000
j	Carrying Cost for Finished Goods	13,000
k	Promotion	800,000
l	Research and Development	800,000
m	Market Research	400,000
n	Economic Research	200,000
o	Misc. Operating Expenses	97,647

4.	TOTAL OPERATING EXPENSES		4,502,412 4.
5.	(3. - 4.) NET INCOME FROM SALES	=	730,088 5.
6.	NET INCOME FROM MARKETABLE SECURITIES	+	7800 6.
7.	TOTAL TAXABLE INCOME (5. + 6.)	=	737,888 7.
8.	INCOME TAXES (.48 x 737,888 7.)	-	354,186 8.
9.	NET INCOME AFTER TAXES (7. - 8.)	=	383,702 9.

Plant book value x .025

CASH FLOW ESTIMATED:

CASH INFLOWS:

A.	SALES REVENUE (1. 11,412,500) =	11,412,500
+B.	SALE OF MARKETABLE SECURITIES	0
+C.	INTEREST FROM MARKETABLE SECURITIES	7800
+D.	NET INCOME TAX CREDIT (if 7. is negative)	0
=E.	TOTAL CASH INFLOW	11,420,300

CASH OUTFLOWS:

F.	PURCHASE OF LEATHER	1,350,000
+G.	PURCHASE OF RUBBER	900,000
+H.	OPERATING EXPENSES REPRESENTING CASH OUTFLOWS:	

a.	3,200,000	h.	135,000
b.	600,000	i.	100,000
c.	341,765	j.	13,000
d.	1,000,000	k.	800,000
e.	0	l.	800,000
f.	100,000	m.	400,000
g.	100,000	n.	200,000
		o.	97647

	SUM OF CASH FLOW OPERATING EXPENSES	7,887,412
+I.	PURCHASE OF MARKETABLE SECURITIES	1,000,000
+J.	DIVIDENDS	25,000
+K.	NET INCOME TAX EXPENSE (if 7. is positive)	354,186
+L.	CAPITAL INVESTMENT	1,000,000
=M.	TOTAL CASH OUTFLOW	12,516,598

NET CASH FLOW

(E. 11,420,000 - M. 12,516,598) = -1,096,298

ESTIMATED CASH BALANCE

	PREVIOUS CASH BALANCE	3,000,000
+	NET CASH FLOW	-1,096,298
	depreciation not included	
=	ESTIMATED CASH BALANCE	1,903,402

Remember that (sales potential) is based on the relative price, promotion, and R & D expenditures of the firm and responds markedly to changes in the seasonal and economic indexes. Additionally, stockouts from the previous period also influence sales potential. After several periods the firms in DECIDE will be able to make relatively accurate estimates of potential sales. One further point to note--a firm may be able to sell more units than it produces for a period because of finished goods that have been produced in previous periods and carried into the current period.

The hypothetical firm projected sales for period 1 of 415,000 (1S) units, which represented the 405,000 units produced during period 1 plus 10,000 in inventory. The remainder of the calculations and estimates are based on actual decisions made by the firm which are determined by calculating values as explained in Chapter 2 or are simply period 0 values. For example, the value for maintenance expenditure of $1,000,000 represents a decision made for this period. The value of $135,000 for the carrying cost of leather is equal to 10% of the period 0 value of ending inventory. The supervisory cost of $341,765 is based on period 0. The value of $13,000 for the carrying cost of finished goods is equal to 10% of the period 0 value of finished goods inventory (see the Balance Sheet).

The resulting estimated income after taxes for period 1 is $383,702 (line 9; Income Statement). The firm conservatively declared a dividend of $25,000, which is slightly less than the recommended 10% of after-tax earnings. Also the firm decided to follow its established strategy of moderate expansion by investing $1,000,000 in capital investment. Since they anticipated depreciation of approximately $415,000 they projected their capacity in labor hours to increase by 9,750 hours for period two (2). This is obtained by utilizing the 60 dollar per unit labor hour conversion factor. That is, capital investment minus depreciation ÷ divided by conversion factor/yields the approximate increased capacity ($1,000,000 − $415,000)/60 = 9750 increased labor capacity.)

The remaining decisions involve the purchase or sale of marketable securities. The purpose of purchasing marketable securities is to invest the excess cash reserves of the firm. In DECIDE, excess cash earns no interest. On completion of the estimated cash inflows from the cash flow statement, the firm determined that $11,420,300 (line E; Cash Flow) would flow into the firm's cash reserves for the period. Based on the cash allocations already determined, an outflow of $11,516,598 was projected. This would result in a negative net cash flow of $96,298. Referring to the period 0 balance sheet, the firm conservatively decided to purchase $1,000,000 of marketable securities increasing their outflow to $12,516,590 (line M; Cash Flow) and projected an ending cash balance of $1,903,402.

DECISIONS OF FIRM #3

To summarize, the firm made the following decisions:

Price —	$27.50
Promotion —	$800,000
R & D —	$800,000
Maintenance —	$1,000,000
Labor Scheduled —	450,000 hours
Leather Ordered —	900,000 sq. ft.
Rubber Ordered —	450,000 sq. ft.
Production —	405,000 units
Dividends —	$25,000
Securities —	$1,000,000 (bought)
Investment —	$1,000,000

// Purchase economic indicators and market research
// pertaining to each firm.

THE SYSTEM

While it is convenient to illustrate the decisions by referring to the three manufacturing functions of marketing, production, and finance, it is imperative for the DECIDE managers to realize the interrelationships of the decisions and the decision making process. Figure 3-4 (page 45) depicts the major interrelationships and reinforces the need for viewing the process in its entirety.

DECISION SHEET

At this point the decisions are encoded on the decision sheet. The decision sheet is set up to facilitate the

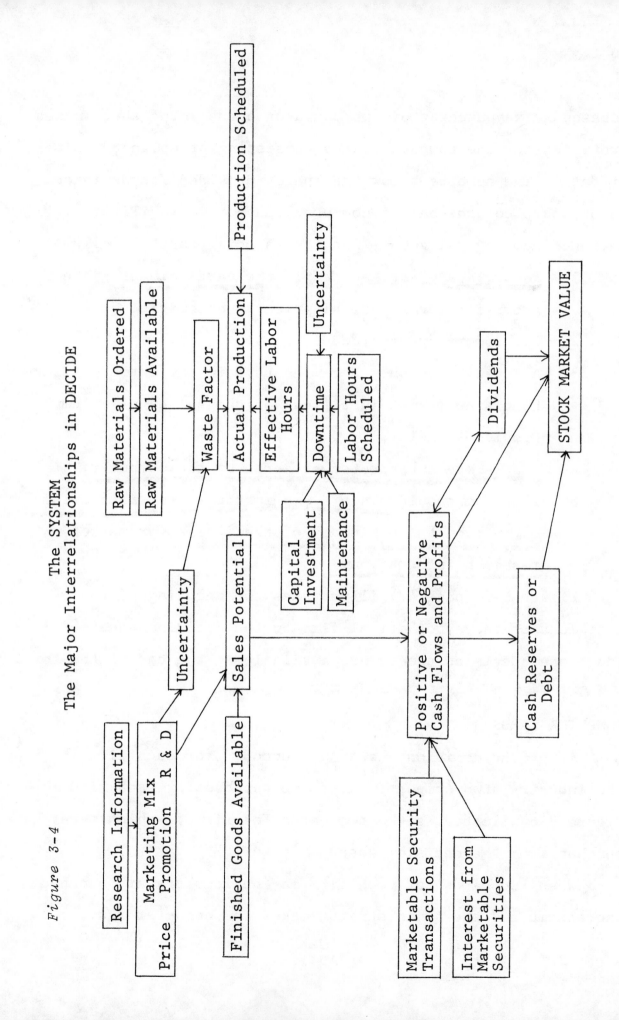

Figure 3-4

The SYSTEM
The Major Interrelationships in DECIDE

subsequent keypunching of two computer cards. The sheet makes
provision for the computer cards consisting of up to 80 columns
of data. The numbers below the spaces provided for decisions
denote card columns on the computer cards. To facilitate
keypunching, several guidelines for encoding must be followed:

1. *Decimals* are *not* encoded in the card columns. The
   provision for a decimal price is automatic.

2. All commas are excluded.

3. All decisions should be recorded in the extreme right-
   hand side (right-justified) of the series of columns
   provided (field).

4. Blanks are interpreted as zeros by the computer.

5. The firm should place a *one* in the appropriate column
   of an item to obtain any of the indexes or market
   research information.

Figure 3-5 (page 47) illustrates the encoding of the
decisions of the hypothetical firm on the decision sheet.
Additional decision sheets are available at the end of the text.

COMPUTER CARDS

After the decision sheets are encoded for each firm in
the industry, two computer cards are punched for each firm.
Figure 3-6 illustrates the two cards for firm #3 which were
punched from the decision sheet. (page 48)

When two cards for each firm in the industry are punched
and assembled, the administrator makes the computer run.

DECISION SHEET

CARD #1

Industry	Firm #	Period #		Price (do not punch decimal)			
5	3	0	1	2	7	5	0
1	2	3	4	5	6	7	8

Promotion (dollars)

	8	0	0	0	0	0
9	10	11	12	13	14	15

R & D (dollars)

	8	0	0	0	0	0
16	17	18	19	20	21	22

Maintenance (dollars)

1	0	0	0	0	0	0
23	24	25	26	27	28	29

Labor Scheduled (hours)   *bottom PJ. 35*

	4	5	0	0	0	0
30	31	32	33	34	35	36

Leather Ordered (sq. ft.)

	9	0	0	0	0	0
37	38	39	40	41	42	43

Rubber Ordered (sq. ft.)   *PJ-35 middle*

	4	5	0	0	0	0
44	45	46	47	48	49	50

Look PJ/1 *PJ 36*

Production Scheduled (units)

	4	0	5	0	0	0
51	52	53	54	55	56	57

Dividends (dollars)

		2	5	0	0	0
58	59	60	61	62	63	64

Securities Bought or Sold (dollars)
(— to sell)

	1	0	0	0	0	0	0
65	66	67	68	69	70	71	72

Investment (dollars)

	1	0	0	0	0	0	0
73	74	75	76	77	78	79	80

CARD #2

5	3	0	1	1	1	1	1	0	1	0	1	0	1	0
1	2	3	4	5	6	7	8	9	10	11	12	13	14	15

Industry	Firm #	Period #	Econ. Index ($75,000)	Seas. Index ($100,000)	Price Index ($25,000)	Price (All) ($100,000)	Price (Mean) ($50,000)	Promotion (All) ($100,000)	Promotion (Mean) ($50,000)	R & D (All) ($100,000)	R & D (Mean) ($50,000)	Sales (All) ($100,000)	Sales (Mean) ($50,000)

Right Justify — Use No Decimals

FIGURE 3-5

Figure 3-6

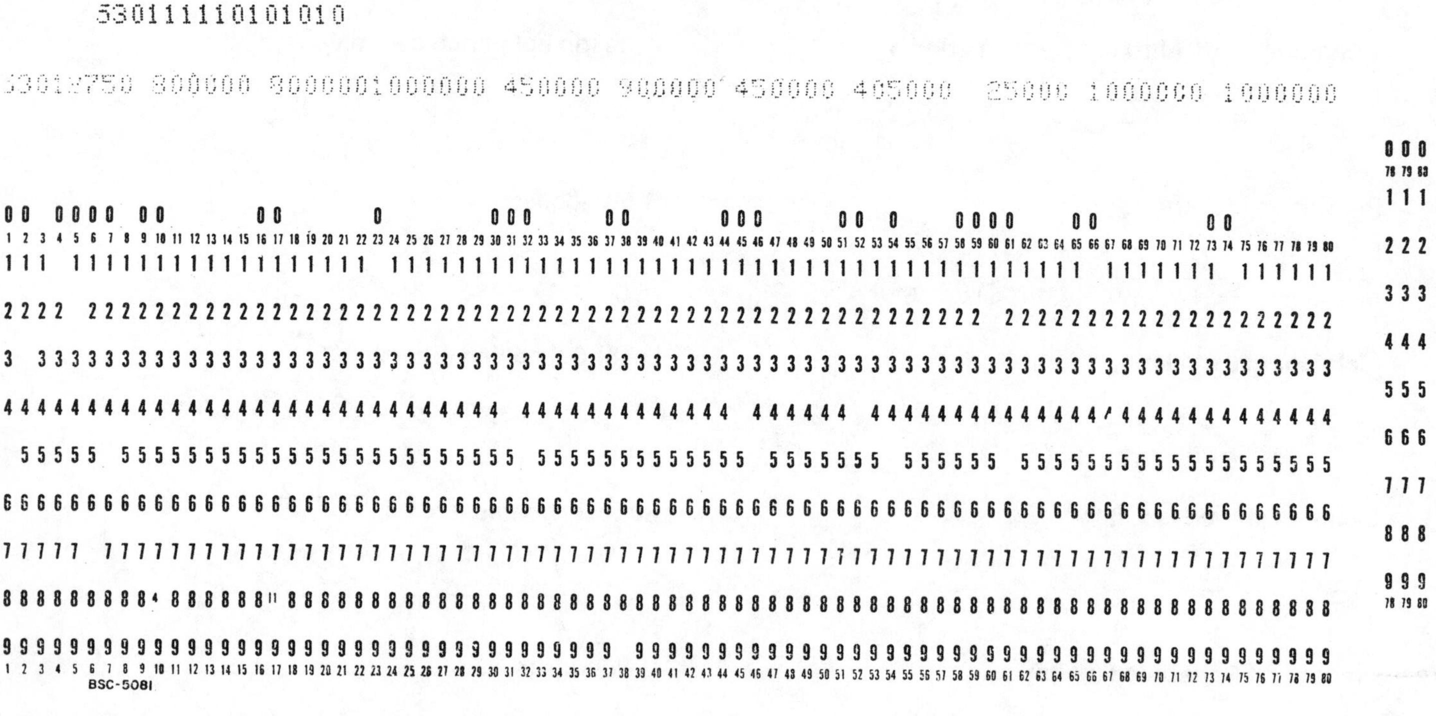

COMPARISON OF PROJECTIONS WITH ACTUAL RESULTS — EX POST ANALYSIS

Once the results for a period are available, it is easier to "look back" at decisions made and isolate errors than to realize that errors are being made during the decision making process. Analyzing decisions in retrospect may reveal systematic errors which may then be eliminated in subsequent periods. It is also useful to compare projections made on the worksheet with the computerized results to locate unexpected occurrences.

The results of team #3's decisions are presented in Figure 3-7. For this special computer run projected estimates from the production and financial worksheets are enclosed in parentheses and appear beside the actual values in the income and cash flow statements. (During the actual simulation, projected estimates *will not* appear on the computer printout.)

RESULTS

Figure 3-7

PROJECTED AND ACTUAL INCOME STATEMENT AND CASH FLOW

INDUSTRY NO. 5
INCOME STATEMENT FOR PERIOD 1 FOR FIRM NO. 3

TOTAL SALES REVENUE (405167. UNITS AT 27.50 PER UNIT)		11142089.	(11,412,500)
COST OF GOODS PRODUCED:			
BEGINNING INVENTORY FINISHED GOODS	130000.	(130,000)	
LABOR (8.00 PER HOUR)	3200000.	(3,200,000)	
OVERTIME PREMIUM	600000.	(600,000)	
LEATHER USED (1.50 PER SQ. FT.)	1302748.	(1,350,000)	
RUBBER USED (2.00 PER SQ. FT.)	878149.	(900,000)	
COST OF GOODS AVAILABLE		6110897.	(6,180,000)
LESS: ENDING INVENTORY FINISHED GOODS		0.	(0)
COST OF GOODS PRODUCED		6110897.	(6,180,000)
GROSS PROFIT		5031192.	(5,232,500)
OPERATING EXPENSES:			
SUPERVISORY	350000.	(341,765)	
MAINTENANCE	1000000.	(1,000,000)	
DEPRECIATION	425000.	(415,000)	
INTEREST EXPENSES	0.	(0)	
ORDERING COST FOR LEATHER	100000.	(100,000)	
ORDERING COST FOR RUBBER	100000.	(100,000)	
CARRYING COST FOR LEATHER	135000.	(135,000)	
CARRYING COST FOR RUBBER	100000.	(100,000)	
CARRYING COST FINISHED GOODS	13000.	(13,000)	
PROMOTION	800000.	(800,000)	
RESEARCH AND DEVELOPMENT	800000.	(800,000)	
MARKET RESEARCH	400000.	(400,000)	
ECONOMIC RESEARCH	200000.	(200,000)	
MISC. OPERATING EXPENSES	100000.	(99,647)	
TOTAL OPERATING EXPENSES		4523000.	(4,502,412)
NET INCOME FROM SALES		508192.	(730,088)
NET INCOME FROM MARKETABLE SECURITIES		7800.	(7,800)
NET TAXABLE INCOME		515992.	(737,888)
INCOME TAXES		247676.	(354,186)
NET INCOME AFTER TAXES		268316.	(383,702)

CASH FLOW STATEMENT FOR PERIOD 1 FOR FIRM NO.3

CASH INFLOWS:		
SALES REVENUE	11142089.	(11,412,500)
SALE OF MARKETABLE SECURITIES	0.	(0)
INTEREST FROM MARKETABLE SECURITIES	7800.	(7,800)
NET INCOME TAX CREDIT	0.	(0)
TOTAL CASH INFLOWS	11149889.	(11,420,300)

CASH OUTFLOWS:

PURCHASE OF LEATHER	1350000.	(1,350,000)
PURCHASE OF RUBBER	900000.	(900,000)
OPERATING EXPENSES REPRESENTING CASH FLOWS	7898000.	(7,887,412)
PURCHASE OF MARKETABLE SECURITIES	1000000.	(1,000,000)
DIVIDENDS	25000.	(25,000)
NET INCOME TAX EXPENSE	247676.	(354,186)
CAPITAL INVESTMENT	1000000.	(1,000,000)
TOTAL CASH OUTFLOWS	12420676.	(12,516,598)
NET CASH FLOW	-1270787.	(- 1,096,298)

INDUSTRY NO. 5

BALANCE SHEET FOR END OF PERIOD 1 FOR FIRM NO. 3

LIABILITIES:

TOTAL LIABILITIES	0.

EQUITY:

BEGINNING EQUITY	23000000.
ADD: NET INCOME	268316.
LESS: DIVIDENDS	25000.
ENDING EQUITY	23243316.
TOTAL LIABILITY + EQUITY	23243316.

ASSETS:

CASH	1729213.
MARKETABLE SECURITIES	1520000.
ENDING INVENTORY:	
LEATHER	1397252.
RUBBER	1021851.
FINISHED GOODS	0.
PLANT BOOK VALUE	17575000.
TOTAL ASSETS	23243316.

SALES SUMMARY FOR PERIOD 1 FOR FIRM NO. 3

	UNITS	DOLLARS
POTENTIAL SALES	572268.	15737378.
ACTUAL SALES	405167.	11142089.
STOCKOUTS	167101.	4595289.

SHARE OF MARKET 25.9 PERCENT

MATERIALS MANAGEMENT REPORT FOR PERIOD 1 FOR FIRM NO. 3

LEATHER:	SQ. FT.
BEGINNING INVENTORY	900000.
PURCHASED	900000.
USED INCLUDING WASTE	868499.
ENDING INVENTORY	931501.

WASTE FACTOR 9.0 PERCENT

RUBBER:	SQ. FT.
BEGINNING INVENTORY	500000.
PURCHASED	450000.
USED INCLUDING WASTE	439074.
ENDING INVENTORY	510926.

WASTE FACTOR 10.0 PERCENT

FINISHED GOODS:	UNITS
BEGINNING INVENTORY	10000.
PRODUCED	395167.
SOLD	405167.
ENDING INVENTORY	0.

LABOR AVAILABILITY AND UTILIZATION REPORT FOR PERIOD 1 FOR FIRM NO. 3

	WITHOUT OVERTIME	WITH OVERTIME
MAXIMUM LABOR HRS. WHICH COULD BE SCHEDULED FOR PERIOD 1	400000.	600000.
ADD: INCREASE DUE TO CAPITAL INVESTMENT	16667.	25000.
LESS: DECREASE DUE TO DEPRECIATION	7083.	10625.
MAXIMUM LABOR HRS. WHICH CAN BE SCHEDULED FOR PERIOD 2	409583.	614375.

ACTUAL HOURS SCHEDULED FOR PERIOD 1	450000.
LESS: DOWNTIME (12.19 PERCENT)	54833.
EFFECTIVE LABOR HOURS	395167.

Actual Production → MACHINERY BREAKDOWN OCCURRED THIS PERIOD

ECONOMIC FORECASTS

SEASONAL INDEX:

PERIOD 1	PERIOD 2	PERIOD 3	PERIOD 4	PERIOD 5	(COST OF RESEARCH IS $100000)
106.	96.	104.	90.	92.	

INDEX OF THE ECONOMY:

PERIOD 1	PERIOD 2	PERIOD 3	PERIOD 4	PERIOD 5	(COST OF RESEARCH IS $75000)
101.	104.	111.	104.	110.	

INFLATION INDEX:

PERIOD 1	PERIOD 2	PERIOD 3	PERIOD 4	PERIOD 5	(COST OF RESEARCH IS $25000)
100.	100.	102.	103.	110.	

INDUSTRY NO. 5
MARKET RESEARCH INFORMATION

STOCK MARKET (NO RESEARCH COST)

FIRM NO.	VALUE	RANK
1	60.79	3
2	61.27	2
3	60.61	4
4	61.70	1

PRICE FOR EACH FIRM (COST OF RESEARCH IS $100000)

FIRM NO.	PRICE
1	25.00
2	26.00
3	27.50
4	28.00

PROMOTION FOR EACH FIRM (COST OF RESEARCH IS $100000)

FIRM NO.	PROMOTION
1	650000.
2	700000.
3	800000.
4	750000.

RESEARCH AND DEVELOPMENT FOR EACH FIRM (COST OF RESEARCH IS $100000)

FIRM NO.	RESEARCH AND DEVELOPMENT
1	450000.
2	500000.
3	800000.
4	500000.

SALES IN UNITS FOR EACH FIRM (COST OF RESEARCH IS $100000)

FIRM NO.	SALES IN UNITS
1	368153.
2	415000.
3	405167.
4	374263.

PRODUCTION AND MATERIALS

From the Materials Management and the Labor Availability and Utilization reports, one can see that actual production was 395,167 units. The unanticipated increase in downtime from 11.24% to 12.19% explains the difference between desired and actual production. Downtime increased due to a machine breakdown (or workstoppage) which is indicated on the computer printout. Due to the restricted production, the amount of raw materials used was less than that projected. In addition, a reduction in the leather waste factor from 10% to 9% reduced the square feet of leather used.

INCOME STATEMENT

The firm was able to sell 405,167 units--the 395,167 produced plus the 10,000 units in finished goods inventory. The firm had projected sales of 415,000 units; therefore, the projected sales revenue was slightly higher than actual sales revenue. The cost of goods produced was lower than projected since fewer raw materials were needed for the restricted production. The estimated operating expenses were very close to the actual operating expenses. The only deviations occurred in the supervisory, depreciation and miscellaneous expenses. These three cost items vary with the size of the plant and inflation.

The actual net income after taxes was $268,316 with $383,102 projected. The deviation is largely attributed to the reduced sales due to the restricted production resulting from the downtime increase.

CASH FLOW STATEMENT

With the exception of the sales revenue, income tax, the supervisory cost and miscellaneous expenses, the projected cash flows and the actual cash flows coincide. The sources of these deviations have been mentioned previously.

PROBLEM AREAS AND UNPREDICTED OCCURRENCES

Although the firm's performance in most categories for the period was satisfactory, there are several problem areas and unexpected occurrences that warrant closer scrutiny.

The firm's potential sales was 572,268 units while the firm had only 405,167 available for sale. This resulted in a stockout of 167,101 units. This means that a significant number of customers were "turned-away" without the goods they desired. Some of these customers may return during the next period, but undoubtedly some will buy goods elsewhere. (See Chapter 4 for additional details on stockouts.) The magnitude of the stockouts is a clear indication of a problem. In retrospect it is clear that the firm was overly aggressive in planning its marketing mix. The price might have been set higher to generate more revenue per unit sold, or the expenditures on promotion and R & D might have been smaller, thereby limiting expenses and thus increasing profits. The firm can refer to the market research information which was purchased and determine that they were clearly the most

54

aggressive with respect to the total marketing mix.

The increase in downtime was due to the expansion program and due in part to some "bad luck" resulting in the occurrence of the machinery breakdown or workstoppages. The capacity of the plant was increased so it is not immediately apparent that the expansion was unwise. The firm might question whether an allocation of $1,000,000 in maintenance was necessary. Careful attention to this expenditure and to downtime is called for in subsequent fiscal periods.

The firm ended the period with a balance of $1,729,213 in cash assets. They had projected a balance of $1,903,402 even with the purchase of $1,000,000 of marketable securities. Clearly, a cash balance of this magnitude is both unnecessary and unwise. For instance, the firm has foregone the opportunity to earn an additional $25,938 per period in interest which would have been realized by the purchase of an additional $1,729,213 of marketable securities. Alternative cash uses such as (i) additional capital expenditures, (ii) larger dividends, (iii) maintenance, (iv) Research and Development expenditures, etc. may also have been desirable.

The remainder of the decisions seem to be at least satisfactory; however, more periods of simulation are necessary to discover their total impact on the firm.

CAUTION:

Although the reader may wish to use the information presented in this chapter as a guideline in developing strategies

for the simulation, the reader is cautioned that the hypothetical
decisions are not necessarily the best decisions. The purpose
of the hypothetical firm has been to acquaint the reader with
procedures and not to reveal a wise or optimal strategy.

SUMMARY

This chapter described the decisions and the results of
a hypothetical firm pursuing a strategy of high price - high
promotion - and maximum production.

The production and financial worksheets, decision forms,
and computer cards were described in general and for team #3,
specifically. The need for understanding the major factors
and interrelationships of the decision variables was stressed.

TERMS AND CONCEPTS OF THE CHAPTER

ex post analysis	maximum production
individual demand factors	decision sheets and computer cards
production worksheet	maximum sales
financial worksheet	actual versus projected
60 dollar labor hour conversion factor	

REVIEW AND DISCUSSION QUESTIONS

1. List three different marketing strategies that a
   team might pursue in DECIDE.

2. How is maximum production determined? Be specific!

3. Why is excess cash unadvisable? How might it be
   reduced?

4. Describe the system illustrated in Figure 3-4.

56

5. List the factors that influence:

   a) downtime percentage
   b) waste percentage
   c) stock market
   d) breakdowns and workstoppages

6. What is the impact on <u>labor capacity</u> in period 2 of a capital investment expenditure of $500,000 in period 1? (Use period 0 results.)

7. Is it possible for downtime to increase significantly when a team spends $3,000,000 on capital investment? Explain your answer.

8. <u>Raw materials used</u> is an estimated figure. What conditions would cause deviations in the estimate?

9. Discuss the possible advantages and disadvantages of the following production alternatives.

   1) Matching production with seasonal swings in demand via overtime.

   2) Smoothing out production over several periods via inventory-building to accommodate seasonal swings.

10. What factors should be considered in forecasting <u>potential sales</u>? How should they be weighted?

Chapter Four:
Special Issues in DECIDE

INTRODUCTION

This chapter considers special issues in DECIDE including (1) uncertainty in forecasts, stockouts, downtime, and the waste factors; (2) interest rates and automatic loans; (3) income tax and its implications, and (4) the components of the stock market function.

This chapter is more technical in nature than the previous three chapters. This chapter is intended to serve as a reference for detailed analytical DECIDE decision making. Understanding all of the material presented in this chapter is *not required* for effective decision making at the outset of the simulation. As the simulation progresses, however, knowledge of the contents of this chapter should improve the manager's decisions.

UNCERTAINTY IN DECIDE

As noted earlier, uncertainty pervades the decision process in DECIDE. It does this through (1) factors primarily external to the firm and (2) factors internal to the operations of the firm.

INDEX FORECASTS — EXTERNAL UNCERTAINTY

The external environment provides uncertainty via the

oligopolistic market structure. In an industry composed of
only a few firms, the major decisions of a firm will not go
unnoticed by its competitors. Thus, even the most effective
DECIDE managers will be confronted with the uncertainty of
how their competitors will respond or react to their decisions.
To cope with this uncertainty the firms may opt to purchase
market information or economic forecasts. The latter, composed
of the index of the economy, the inflation index, and the
seasonal index, are useful for future production planning.
The forecasts themselves are subject to uncertainty. The
degree of uncertainty increases as the teams attempt to
forecast further into the future. The following table illustrates
the maximum error contained in the DECIDE forecasts for the
indexes:

Table 4-1

*Maximum Error in
Forcast Information**

Forecast

Index	Next Period	Two Periods Hence	Three Periods Hence	Four Periods Hence
Seasonal	± 2	± 10	± 15	± 20
Economy	± 2	± 5	± 7	± 9
Inflation	± 2	± 4	± 5	± 6

*All figures represent possible index point deviations
from the "real" values.

Reference to Table 4-1 indicates that the seasonal index
is the most uncertain while the inflation index has the least

"noise" (i.e. the least uncertainty). To illustrate, if the actual Index of Economy for the next four periods was 100, 101, 102, 103, respectively, the forecasted values would fall in the following ranges:

Table 4-2

True versus the Range of Predicted
DECIDES Forecast for the
Index of the Economy

	Next Period	Two Periods Hence	Three Periods Hence	Four Periods Hence
True Index of the Economy	100	101	102	103
Range of DECIDE Forecasted values for the Index of the Economy	(98 to 102)	(96 to 106)	(95 to 109)	(94 to 112)

Each period the specific forecasted values for all three indexes are selected by the computer randomly but are constrained to the applicable range. The average forecasted value will center on the actual value (i.e. the expected value of the forecasted value is equal to the actual value).

UNCERTAINTY — INTERNAL FACTORS

Uncertainty is also introduced into internal operations of the firm through factors such as (i) impact of stockouts on sales potential, (ii) downtime and workstoppages in the production process, and (iii) the effectiveness of research and development on waste factor reduction. Once again the computer generates the uncertainty randomly but within a constrained range.

While the DECIDE managers cannot control the specific random selections, they can in some cases influence the range of possible selection alternatives. The technical aspects of the uncertainty factors and the computer random generator are described below in detail.

STOCKOUTS

As in the "real world," sales dollars and revenues are usually lost when consumers are unable to purchase desired products. Questions that plague both retailers and wholesalers include: What proportion of the total stockouts will return to the firm? What proportion will go to the competitors?

In DECIDE, the *maximum* number of returning stockouts for each firm is *50%* of their stockouts from the previous period. However, the actual value is determined by the computer random generator within the limits of 0 to 50%. The following illustrates how the DECIDE program calculates returning sales from the previous period's stockouts:

Suppose that Firm J stocked out by 50,000 units in period 3. Then their MAXIMUM POTENTIAL RETURN would be 25,000 units for period 4. However, the actual number of returning sales is dependent upon the value of the random number. (The random numbers vary from 0 to 1.00 with an equal probability of occurence.) If the computer generated a value of .1, then this firm would only receive 2,500 return sales (MAXIMUM POTENTIAL RETURN times computer generator value); while if the value were .8, the firm would receive 20,000 return sales.[1]

The stockouts which are not returned to the firm are added to the total industry demand and are allocated to *all* firms by way of the forces of supply and demand.

DOWNTIME AND WORKSTOPPAGES

In DECIDE a firm may increase its level of operations through capital investment. However, rapid expansion generates associated costs. Part of these costs are reflected in workstoppages due to problems of material flow and the diversion of production employees to new machinery set up duties. The net effect is increased downtime potential.

A second cause of increased downtime is machinery breakdown. Machinery breakdowns occur due to (i) inadequate maintenance and (ii) inadequate capital replacement programs.

Each of the primary causes of increased downtime are explained in detail through the use of numerical examples below.

INADEQUATE PREVENTATIVE MAINTENANCE — IMPACT OF DOWNTIME

Expenditures in maintenance help prevent breakdowns and thus may prevent increases in downtime. Increased downtime may occur if a firm fails to adequately associate maintenance expenditures with production levels. An excessive preventative maintenance program may not reduce downtime significantly because diminishing returns set in.

---

[1] Based on expected value concept, DECIDE managers should anticipate return sales at 25% of the total previous period stockouts.

62

To illustrate: Given that a firm has an inherent 10%
downtime factor, a plant capacity of 600,000 units (full overtime), and a production level of 400,000 units, the effects
of various maintenance decisions on downtime are shown in
Table 4-3, below.

Table 4-3

Maintenance Related to Downtime
with Production at 400,000 Units

Maintenance Decision (in dollars)	Impact of Maintenance Decision on Downtime (%)	Resulting Downtime Percentage[2]
0	+ 8.71	18.71
50,000	+ 7.83	17.83
200,000	+ 4.07	14.07
400,000	+ 0.79	10.79
600,000	+ 0.00	10.00
1,000,000	+ 0.00	10.00

As the production level approaches plant capacity, downtime
will increase unless a proper preventative maintenance policy
is implemented. For the above examples with a production level
of *500,000 units:*

Table 4-4

Maintenance Related to Downtime
with Production at 500,000 Units

Maintenance Decision (in dollars)	Impact of Maintenance Decision on Downtime (%)	Resulting Downtime Percentage[2]
0	+ 16.67	26.67
50,000	+ 16.34	26.34
400,000	+ 2.78	12.78

[2]This assumes that all other decisions influencing downtime would
not increase or decrease downtime percentage from the initial 10%
base.

INADEQUATE CAPITAL REPLACEMENT — IMPACT ON DOWNTIME

If a firm fails to replace worn out and depreciated equipment on a regular basis, the firm risks potential increases in downtime. These increases in downtime (due to machinery breakdowns) can be severe due to the fact that certain machines may represent "bottlenecks" in the production process. Both the risk of a breakdown and the severity of the breakdown are subject to the computer random number generator contained in DECIDE's source program. An example of the increased risk associated with failure to replace depreciated capital equipment is presented in Table 4-5.

Table 4-5

*Capital Investment Related to Probability
of a Breakdown with
Depreciation Expense of $400,000*

Capital Investment Decision (in dollars)	Depreciation Expense minus Investment (in dollars)	Probability of a Breakdown (as a decimal)[3]
0	400,000	.480
100,000	300,000	.382
200,000	200,000	.275
300,000	100,000	.159
400,000	0	.000

Once the probability of a breakdown has been determined, a random number is generated. The value of the random number generated is compared with the probability of a breakdown. If the random number is *less than* the probability, then a breakdown occurs. If it is *greater than* or *equal to*, no

---

[3] The formula used is: Probability = [(Depreciation — Investment)/10^6].8

machinery breakdown occurs. In the case of a breakdown, the magnitude of the breakdown in terms of increased downtime is equal to the value of the random number generated. To illustrate the above, two examples are shown. The first assumes a random number generated value of .36; the second assumes a value of .158.

Based upon Table 4-5 and assuming an inherent 10% downtime factor, the effect of various investment decisions on downtime is shown in Table 4-6.

Table 4-6

Capital Investment Related to Downtime
with a Random Number of .36

Capital Investment Decision (in dollars)	Depreciation Expense minus Investment (in dollars)	Probability of a Breakdown (as a decimal)	Impact of a Breakdown on Downtime (%)	Resulting Downtime Percentage[4]
0	400,000	.480	+ 36	46.0
100,000	300,000	.382	+ 36	46.0
200,000	200,000	.275	+ 0	10.0
300,000	100,000	.159	+ 0	10.0
400,000	0	.000	+ 0	10.0

It is important to note that if the generated random number exceeded .48 no breakdown would have occurred. Thus, even with no capital investment the resulting downtime would have been 10%.

Based on Table 4-5 and assuming an inherent 10% downtime factor, the effect of various investment decisions on downtime

---

[4]This assumes that all other decisions influencing downtime will not increase or decrease the downtime percentage. The resulting downtime percentage is the sum of the inherent 10% downtime factor and the breakdown magnitude.

is shown in Table 4-7.

Table 4-7

Capital Investment Related to Downtime
with a Random Number of .158

Capital Investment Decision (in dollars)	Depreciation Expense minus Investment (in dollars)	Probability of a Breakdown (as a decimal)	Impact of a Breakdown on Downtime (%)	Resulting Downtime Percentage[5]
0	400,000	.480	+ 15.8	25.8
100,000	300,000	.382	+ 15.8	25.8
200,000	200,000	.275	+ 15.8	25.8
300,000	100,000	.043	+ 0	10.0
400,000	0	.000	+ 0	10.0

OVERZEALOUS CAPITAL EXPANSION — IMPACT ON DOWNTIME

Rapid expansion bears the risk of increased chances of workstoppages and thus increased downtime. The risk of workstoppages and the severity of the workstoppages are influenced by the random number generator in DECIDE. An example of the increased *risk* associated with rapid expansion is presented in Table 4-8. Given that the company has a plant book value of $17,000,000 and that the following capital expenditures were made, the increase in the chances for workstoppages are as follows:

---

[5]This analysis assumes all other decisions influencing the the downtime percentage have not increased or decreased the downtime percentage. The resulting downtime is based upon inadequate capital replacement and the inherent 10% downtime factor. The resulting downtime for this example is merely the sum of the breakdown magnitude and the inherent 10% factor.

Table 4-8

*Capital Investment Related to
Probability of a Workstoppage
with a Depreciation Expense of $425,000*

Capital Investment Decision (in dollars)	Investment minus Depreciation (in dollars)	Probability of a Workstoppage (%)[6]
1,000,000	575,000	10.2
3,000,000	2,575,000	33.8
10,000,000	9,575,000	96.6
20,000,000	19,575,000	100.0

Once the probability of a workstoppage has been determined a random number is generated. The value of the random number generated is compared with the probability of a workstoppage. If it is *greater than* or *equal to*, no workstoppages will occur. In the case of workstoppage, the magnitude of the stoppage in terms of *increased* downtime is *equal to* the value of the random number generated. To illustrate the above relationship two examples are shown. The first assumes a random generated value of .31; the second assumes a value of .72.

Based on Table 4-8 and assuming an inherent 10% downtime factor, the effect of various investment decisions on downtime is shown in Table 4-9.

---

[6]The formula used to calculate the probability is as follows:
Probability = $[(\text{Investment} - \text{Depreciation})/10^7]^{.8}$

Table 4-9

Capital Investment Related to Downtime
with a Random Number of .31

Capital Investment (in dollars)	Probability of a Workstoppage (as a decimal)	Impact of Workstoppage on Downtime (%)	Resulting[7] Downtime (%)
1,000,000	.102	+ 0.0	10.0
3,000,000	.338	+ 31.0	41.0
10,000,000	.966	+ 31.0	41.0
20,000,000	1.000	+ 31.0	41.0

For the second example, Table 4-10, it is assumed that the firm received a random number of .72 towards overzealous capital intensification downtime.

Table 4-10

Capital Investment Related to Downtime
with a Random Number of .72

Capital Investment (in dollars)	Probability of a Workstoppage (as a decimal)	Impact of Workstoppage on Downtime (%)	Resulting[7] Downtime (%)
1,000,000	.102	+ 0.0	10.0
3,000,000	.338	+ 0.0	10.0
10,000,000	.966	+ 72.0	82.0
20,000,000	1.000	+ 72.0	82.0

For the second example, if the firm had received a small random number (say .05) then the firm would have incurred workstoppages for any of the capital investment decisions presented. This small random number represents "luck" for

---

[7] This analysis assumes all other decisions influencing the downtime percentage have not increased or decreased the downtime percentage. The resulting downtime is based on overzealous capital intensification and the inherent 10% downtime factor. The resulting downtime is merely the sum of inherent downtime factor of 10% and the workstoppage magnitude.

the firm, because its downtime would have only increased to 10.05%. If the firm had received a large random number, say .97, the firm would not have incurred workstoppages for capital expenditures of less than $10,000,000.

REDUCED DOWNTIME VIA PLANNED CAPITAL EXPANSION

Up to this point, no mention has been made of the process through which a firm may reduce the downtime percentage below the inherent 10% figure. DECIDE incorporates the philosophy that newer capital equipment is more efficient and productive than older vintages of equipment. Thus, it is possible to reduce the downtime percentage through a planned capital intensification program. Table 4-11 illustrates how a firm might reduce the inherent 10% downtime factor through expanding its plant overtime.

Table 4-11

*Reduced Downtime via Planned Capital Intensification
with the Inherent Downtime of 10 Percent*

Plant Book Value (in dollars)	Reduction Factor[8] (as a decimal)	Resulting Downtime[9] (%)
17,000,000	1.000	10.00
17,500,000	.956	9.56
18,000,000	.914	9.14
18,500,000	.887	8.87
19,000,000	.836	8.36
25,000,000	.504	5.04
30,000,000	.345	3.45

---

[8] The formula used to calculate the reduction factor is as follows: Reduction Factor = .90 X [$e^{-A \text{ Factor}}$] + .1 where A Factor = [Plant Book Value + Investment − 17,000,000 − Depreciation]/10^7

[9] This analysis assumes all other decisions influencing the downtime factor have not increased or decreased the downtime factor. For this example the resulting downtime percentage is merely the product of the reduction factor and the inherent downtime percentage.

DOWNTIME — A COMPREHENSIVE EXAMPLE

To illustrate how the downtime percentage is determined, the following example is based upon the history for period 0 (Table 1-1, pages 10 ff.) and the decisions for period 1 for a hypothetical firm are presented. From period 0 and period 1 the following information is obtained.

History: For Period 0

Plant Book Value	$17,000,000
Depreciation	425,000
Maximum Labor Hours Scheduled (plant capacity)	600,000 units

Decisions: For Period #1
Assume the team made the following decisions for period #1.

Investment	$2,000,000
Maintenance	350,000
Production Decision	600,000 units

Random Number: For Period #1
Assume the team received a random number of .500.

THE DECISIONS AND CALCULATION OF DOWNTIME

The maintenance decision of $350,000 is clearly inadequate (as indicated by Table 4-3 and Table 4-4 on page 62). The increase in downtime would have been 9.1% if all other downtime factors were held constant. They were not. The other major decision included a large capital investment.

CAPITAL EXPANSION

Since the team replaced the wornout equipment (i.e. their investment exceeded the depreciation by $1,575,000) there was no chance for machinery breakdown because of faulty capital equipment.

However, since the firm had a net capital investment of
$1,575,000, which expanded its output potential by 26,250
units (i.e. [$1,575,000]/60) it incurred a risk of increased
downtime due to workstoppages. The probability of a workstoppage
is 22.79% (see Table 4-8, page 66, footnote 6). Based on the
assumption that the team received a random number of .500,
the firm experienced favorable luck and did not incur increased
downtime because of its investment decision.

Furthermore, since the firm increased its plant book
value by purchasing new equipment, it will reduce the downtime. The reduction factor for newer equipment was .8688
(see Table 4-11, page 68, footnote 9).

DOWNTIME DETERMINATION

To illustrate how the final downtime percentage is obtained,
the following variables are defined:

Reduce = The reduction factor (in this case .8688).

Maint = The increase in downtime due to inadequate
         maintenance (in this case .091).

Base   = The inherent 10% downtime factor (in all cases
         .10).

Cap   = The increase in downtime either due to inadequate
         capital replacement *or* to overzealous capital
         expansion (in this case 0.0).

The downtime percentage is calculated by Equation 4-1.

(4-1) Downtime Percentage = [Base + Maint + Cap] X Reduce

For this problem:

Downtime Percentage = [.10 + .091 + 0.0] X .8688 = .1659

Thus, this team would have had 16.59% downtime factor for period 1. Part of the increase due to the inadequate maintenance decision was reduced because of the effectiveness of newer equipment that was installed.

REDUCTION IN WASTE FACTORS

Spending money on R & D may reduce the waste associated with the production of a product. However, there is a certain amount of luck involved in the innovative process. Sometimes R & D expenditures may lead to cost reduction techniques while other times they may not.

In DECIDE, for a firm to receive the benefits of R & D via waste reduction, they must satisfy the following criteria:[10]

I.   Spend, on the average over time, more than their competitors for R & D.[11] Criterion I *qualifies* the firm for a possible breakthrough on waste reduction. Whether a breakthrough occurs is a function of the random number generator. The second criterion necessary to obtain a cost reduction is:

II.   Receive a random number of less than or equal to .500. Assuming both criteria are fulfilled, the team's waste

[10] R & D serves twin purposes in DECIDE: (i) it differentiates the product (thus increasing the demand for the product) and (ii) enables the firm to produce the product with less waste. The first (i) component of R & D effectiveness occurs under conditions of certainty (i.e. each dollar spent will influence the team's demand curve), whereas the second (ii) component occurs under conditions of uncertainty (i.e. waste reduction is not guaranteed even if the firm spends enormous amounts on R & D).

[11] This is actually a weighted average of past R & D expenditures where exponential smoothing is used to do the weighting. The weighting process is approximately equivalent to a three-period moving average of R & D expenditures.

factor is reduced by Equation 4-2.

(4-2) New Waste Percentage = Old Waste Percentage X .90.

If a team satisfies Criterion I, then the firm has two chances to receive a breakthrough and reduce waste. The random number generator generates two unique random numbers. One number pertains to the leather waste factor and the other to the rubber waste factor percentage. Thus, it is possible to have a breakthrough for *either* rubber *or* leather, *or* both. It is important to note that each time a team receives an R & D breakthrough for either product or both, the respective waste factor is reduced to .90 times the previous percentage, and this new waste percentage lasts for the entirety of the game or until another breakthrough occurs.

AUTOMATIC LOANS AND THE INTEREST RATE

The DECIDE program provides automatic loans to firms. If a firm experiences a net cash outflow in excess of its cash reserves, money is automatically loaned to the firm. Under these circumstances, the balance sheet for the firm will show a zero balance of Cash and a positive balance in Liabilities. Subsequent net cash outflows will increase the total liability; net cash inflows will decrease the liability. The loan is provided automatically and the repayment of the loan is also automatic when the firm generates net cash inflows.

Is it bad for a firm to borrow money (i.e. to have liabilities)? The answer to this question is dependent on the answer to two additional and related questions:

1. Is there a legitimate need for additional cash (i.e.
    will the additional capital significantly increase
    the earnings of the firm)?

2. What is the cost of borrowing?

It is not possible to generalize an answer to the first
question. DECIDE managers are left to determine the benefits
of the additional capital. Borrowing is the norm for contemporary
corporations; therefore, it can be concluded that borrowing is
not categorically bad.

As to the second question, the cost of borrowing is
dependent upon the total amount borrowed (i.e. total liability).
In DECIDE, small amounts of liability (i.e. less than $1,000,000)
incur an interest rate of about 10% annually. However, as
the total liability increases, the interest rate increases.
The rationale is that a firm becomes a greater risk to the
creditors as the total liability increases. The institutions
that loan the money are cognizant of the additional risk and,
therefore, reflect this in the effective interest rate. Figure
4-1 (page 74) shows the relationship between the total liability
of a DECIDE firm and the annual interest rate charged.

Thus, it becomes apparent that a firm which incurs a
large debt will suffer significant increases in its operating
expenses because of the prohibitive interest charges. Careful
cash flow analysis is one of the prerequisites for financial
success in DECIDE.

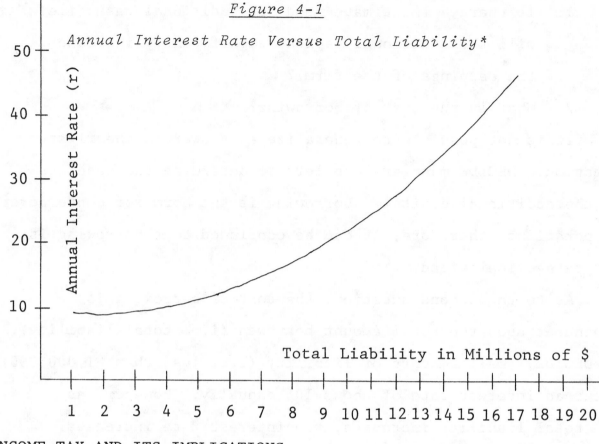

Figure 4-1

Annual Interest Rate Versus Total Liability*

Annual Interest Rate (r)

Total Liability in Millions of $

INCOME TAX AND ITS IMPLICATIONS

In DECIDE the income tax rate is 48%, which is representative of real world situations. Some of the implications of the income taxes are apparent and some are not. For each $1 of taxable income generated by a firm, the government deducts 48¢ if the firm is profitable. What if the firm is not profitable (i.e. loses money)? In DECIDE if a firm loses money the effect of net taxes is a reduction in the loss incurred. To illustrate, if a firm loses $100,000 before taxes, the after tax loss would be $52,000. In DECIDE it appears that the government has absorbed 48% of the loss. In addition, there would be an

* The formula used to calculate the interest rate is:
$$r = [(2.0\ e^{(\text{total debt}/10^7)} + .5)/100]\ X\ 4.00$$

associated cash inflow of $48,000. While this is a simplifying assumption, in the real world losses realized in a particular period can be charged against subsequent periods and the resulting effect is virtually the same as the DECIDE expedient.

A more subtle question is, what does it really cost when the firm spends $1? While the answer would seem to be $1, let's look more closely at the question. Firms are in business to realize profits, specifically profits after taxes. The question might then be restated: What are the after tax implications of an expenditure of one dollar? A simple example may serve to answer the question. Assume a firm with a simplified income statement as shown below:

Revenue	$10.00
Expenses	- 8.00
Taxable Income	2.00
Taxes at 48%	- .96
Income after Tax	$ 1.04

Now let's follow through the implications of the firm spending an additional $1 on a tax deductible expense such as promotion. One might expect an increase in revenue but to be conservative let's follow through the minimal effect with no change in revenue. See the revised income statement below with $1 added to the expenses.

Revenue	$10.00	
Expenses	- 9.00	($8.00 plus $1.00 added)
Taxable Income	1.00	
Taxes at 48%	- .48	
Income after Tax	$ .52	

By comparing incomes after taxes in the initial situation and the revised, one can observe that the income taxes were reduced by $.48 and that the income after tax decreased by $.52 instead of by $1. The reduction of $1 occurred in taxable income but the income tax effect reduced the cost to $.52 after taxes.

The equation for the effect can be shown to be:

(4-3) Before Tax Cost X (1 - Tax Rate) = After Tax Cost

This illustration can be generalized to the DECIDE simulation and carries this important message to DECIDE managers: each dollar spent on tax deductible expenses in DECIDE costs only $.52 in after taxes.

STOCK MARKET FUNCTION

The performance of a firm can be judged based on many factors (i.e. sales, share of market, profits, costs, etc.). In DECIDE the relative performance of firms is based on their stock market price. All firms in DECIDE start with identical assets and a stock market price of $60. Presumably the performance of the firms will affect the stock market prices in a rational manner and, therefore, will be measured by their stock market price.

There are numerous models that purport to be useful in predicting a firm's stock market price. The stock market price function in DECIDE is not meant to be illustrative or be based on the "best" of these models. The DECIDE stock market function is based on three components in the determination of a firm's stock price.

The three component factors of the DECIDE stock market price are: 1) earnings pattern; 2) debt; 3) dividend policy. Each period these three factors are evaluated and combined to determine the marginal (period) impact on the cumulative stock market price. The stock market price as of the end of any period is determined by combining the period impact on stock price and the historical (i.e. previous) stock market price. To illustrate, let us assume for the first period that after evaluating the three component factors the period impact on stock price is determined to be $70. The $70 period impact and the $60 historical stock price are combined with the equation 4-4 below to result in a *stock price of $61.*

$$(4\text{-}4) \quad SP^*_t = (a) \times (SP_t) + (1 - a) \times (SP^*_{t-1})$$

Where SP^*_t = the exponentially smoothed stock price for period t.

SP_t = period impact on stock price based on three component factors.

SP^*_{t-1} = exponentially smoothed stock price for previous period. (Assumed to be $60 for first period and calculated thereafter.)

a = exponential smoothing coefficient. (Assumed to be .1 for the first period.)

Thus, for the first period, the calculation of stock price using the equation would be:

$61 = (.1) \times (70) + (1 - .1) \times (60).$

The $61 stock price is stored as history and will represent the historical stock price in period 2.

In addition, the smoothing coefficient (a) changes over time as indicated below.

Period	Smoothing Coefficient
1	.1
2	.2
3	.3
4	.4
5	.4

In the fourth and all subsequent periods a = .4.

The effect of the small "a" value in early periods is to dampen the impact of management errors in early play on the stock market value. The intent of this feature is to encourage firms to experiment initially, and to "learn by doing."

THREE COMPONENT FACTORS OF PERIOD IMPACT ON STOCK MARKET PRICE

1. Earnings — This factor is based on the amount and the timing of earnings (i.e. net income after tax). This factor can have either a negative or positive impact on the stock price.

   A series of calculations are performed on the earnings to determine the rate of return for the firm. The concept of rate of return is analogous to the percentage interest received for money invested. In general, the higher the return the better the investment.

   To determine the effect of the earnings on the stock

price, the following adjustment is made to recognize
that money has a "time value" (i.e. money earned in
the early stages of the simulation is more valuable
because it can be reinvested). After these adjust-
ments are made the rate of return is calculated.
The resulting rate of return is compared with a chosen
standard of 8% annually. If the firm's rate of
return exceeds 8% then there will be a positive
influence on the stock price. If the rate is less
than 8% there will be a negative influence. The
magnitude of the influence is a function of the
deviation from 8%.

Let's reconsider the above in more simplistic terms.
Each DECIDE team begins with $23,000,000 in assets.
If the management liquidated all assets and deposited
the money in a bank, they would expect a certain
return (interest rate). The deposits in the bank
would be relatively secure and, therefore, probably
pay a lower return than other more speculative
investments. Thus, the 8% which was selected as a
standard indicates a recognition that if the firm
does not liquidate, its rate of return should exceed
the secure bank interest rate. If one multiplies
8% times the $23,000,000 and then divides by 4, the
resulting $460,000 is the standard. Thus, a firm
must achieve an average earnings of $460,000 per

period after tax in order to insure a positive impact
on the stock price.

2. <u>Debt (liability)</u> — The second factor which influences
    the stock price each period is the impact of debt
    (liability). The influence of debt is either negative
    or zero. The calculation of this influence involves
    a comparison made between the rate of return and the
    interest rate paid for debt which was described in
    Figure 4-1, page 74. If the firm has borrowed no
    additional funds then there is no debt influence. If
    the firm has borrowed excessively, the interest rate
    on debt will exceed the rate of return on earnings
    and the firm's stock price will be affected negatively.
    If the firm has borrowed modest amounts and used the
    money judiciously, the benefits are *not* incorporated
    in the debt factor but will be realized in increased
    earnings.

3. <u>Dividend Policy</u> — The final component considered in
    the DECIDE stock price valuation is the firm's divi-
    dend policy. Economists and financial analysts have
    advanced numerous theories that hypothesize the in-
    fluence of dividend on the stock price. There is no
    general concensus as to the dividend policy that
    can be expected to maximize stock price. One theory
    suggests that shareholders expect to receive a certain

share of the earnings of the corporation during the period of time in which the earnings are generated. The participants in DECIDE are advised to assume that the shareholders react most positively if the firm adopts the policy of declaring dividends of 10% of the period earnings during good periods and at least $25,000 during bad periods.

The influence of dividend policy on stock price can be either positive or negative. A Firm realizing low earnings of significantly deviating from the recommended 10% will realize a negative influence on stock price. A firm that accurately projects its earnings and that follows the prescribed dividend policy will receive a positive influence provided that earnings are sufficiently large. The key to successful dividend policy is contingent on accurate projection of earnings.

Each period the three component factors (earnings, debt, and dividend policy) are evaluated, their influences are quantified and combined with the historical stock price (via the exponential smoothing process described previously), and the stock price is determined.

82

SUMMARY

This chapter indicates the pervasiveness of uncertainty in DECIDE. While managers cannot control all of the components of uncertainty, they can minimize, in some cases, the unfavorable repercussions of it.

The technical aspects of stockouts, downtime, and waste factor considerations were described in detail. The automatic loan and interest rate functions were analyzed. Implications of tax deductible expenses and the components of the stock market function were discussed.

TERMS AND CONCEPTS OF THE CHAPTER

time value of money	"noise"
random number generator	reduction factor
expected value	criterion I and II
inherent 10% downtime factor	period impact
workstoppage	after tax cost
"bottleneck"	exponential smoothing

REVIEW AND DISCUSSION QUESTIONS

1. How does the firm experience external uncertainty?

2. Which of the forecasted indexes is the least reliable? Which is most reliable? Can you suggest a reason why this is so?

3. Can an inadequate maintenance decision cause downtime to double? Explain.

4. If your firm stocked out in period 1 by 50,000 units, what is the most reasonable expectation for the number of stockouts returning to your firm in period 2? Explain.

5. If your firm's total debt was $17,000,000, what would be the effective annual interest charge?

6. Is it possible to have both cash and liabilities at the same time?

7. If you receive 3 consecutive R & D breakthroughs in leather, what would be the leather waste factor percentage? (Assume initial 10% waste.)

8. "A firm that incurs a debt of two million dollars is insured of a declining stock market price in DECIDE." Comment.

9. What is the maximum potential downtime that a firm could realize? Explain in detail how this could occur.

10. Explain the implication of the changing exponential smoothing coefficient (a) on the stock market function. Under what circumstances may this have a detrimental effect? A beneficial effect?

Index and Glossary of Terms

Appendix I:
A Discussion of Accounting Statements and Management Reports

A DISCUSSION OF THE ACCOUNTING STATEMENTS AND MANAGEMENT REPORTS

This section is designed to acquaint those students with no previous training with the Accounting and Management Reports used in DECIDE. Although many aspects of these reports are self-explanatory, some coverage of the technical aspects will assist the DECIDE manager in interpreting the computer results. The intent of this section is not to explain in detail the intricacies of these statements but rather to alleviate some of the frequently encountered problems in using and interpreting them. In addition, the origin within the firm of each of the statements is explained.

The Income Statement, Cash Flow Statement, and Balance Sheet are three of the statements that are typically developed by the accounting departments of firms on a regular basis.

INCOME AND CASH FLOW STATEMENTS

Students frequently are confused by the similarities and subtle differences between the income and cash flow statements. Some similarities include the facts that (i) both are reported for a specified period of time (e.g. a fiscal quarter or year) and (ii) both represent gauges by which the performance of the firm can be measured.

Income Statement — The income statement (See Table 1-1, pages 10ff.) is composed of (i) a section in which revenue from sales is reported, (ii) a section reflecting the cost of producing goods, and (iii) a section of operating expenses. Multiple columns are used to permit the account-ant to report subtotals as well as totals. The general format of the income statement is *revenue* minus *cost of goods produced* equals *gross profit*; minus *operating expenses* equals *net income from sales*. *Net income plus* income from *interest* from marketable securities *yields* total *taxable income*. Taxes at a percentage rate of 48% are subtracted yielding net income after taxes (See Figure A1-1).

Figure A1-1

DECIDE Income Statement

```
  Sales Revenue
- Cost of Goods Produced
  Gross Profit
- Operating Expenses
  Net Income from Sales
+ Interest from Marketable Securities
  Total Taxable Income
- Income Taxes (48%)
  Net Income after Taxes
```

Cash Flow Statement — The cash flow statement (See Table 1-1, page 10) is composed of (i) a section in which cash inflows from all sources are reported, (ii) a section in which cash outflows are reported, and (iii) the net cash flow which is the difference between the totals for inflows and outflows.

Many students have the impression that an income statement and a cash flow statement are virtually synonymous; this often leads to confusion. The similarities are pointed out above. The basis for these differences stems from the fact that some items affecting net income are not cash flow items and some cash flow items do not affect net income. It is important that one appreciate the difference between a cash flow and a non-cash flow. It is helpful to imagine a firm that keeps all of its cash (i.e. checks, coins and paper currency) in a vault. Any transaction that would require that someone physically take cash from the vault or place cash in the vault would be a transaction representing a cash flow. To illustrate, if one sold merchandise and received cash in payment, this would be a positive cash flow transaction and a positive income. Although there is no provision for credit sales in DECIDE, it is useful to consider the effect of sales on credit. These sales do not represent cash flows but do represent increases in income.

To illustrate another instance in which cash flow and income differ, consider the effect of depreciation of machinery. This depreciation is an expense and, therefore, affects income. No payment is made from the hypothetical vault and, therefore, this does not represent a cash flow.

Students typically anticipate that a positive income
for a period will be matched with a positive net cash flow
for a period and vice versa. There is no compelling reason
for both income and cash flow to move in the same direction.
Consider an instance in which the firm makes a positive
income for a period and buys a substantial amount of
marketable securities. The purchase of marketable securities
does not represent an expense and, therefore, is not
reported in the income statement but does represent a cash
outflow. As a consequence a net cash outflow might result.
One can logically reverse this relationship by envisioning
a firm with a loss of income that sells marketable securities.
This could result in a positive cash inflow and a negative
income.

A schematic diagram showing cash flow is presented in
Figure A1-2 (page 95).

BALANCE SHEET

The balance sheet (See Table 1-1, page 10) is the third
type of statement which is generated on a regular basis by the
accounting department of a firm. It is based on the fundamental
equation of accounting that states:

$$\text{Assets} = \text{Liabilities} + \text{Owner Equity}$$

The easiest way to conceptualize a balance sheet is to imagine
that at some point in time (usually the end of the fiscal quarter
or year) you took a snapshot of the entire plant and all contents.

Figure A1-2

Schematic Cash Flow

Inflow

+

Outflow

-

Vault

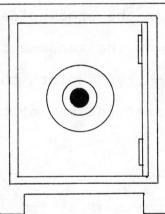

+ Sales
Revenue

+ Sales and
Interest from
Marketable
Securities

+ Net Income
Tax Credit

- Purchase of
Raw Materials

- Operating Expenses
Representing
Cash Flow

- Purchase of
Marketable
Securities

- Dividends

- Net Income
Tax Expenses

- Capital
Investment

The assets are everything of value that would be captured in
the snapshot. In DECIDE this end of the period snapshot would
include the cash, marketable securities, leather, rubber
finished goods and the plant itself. In order to establish
a dollar value of assets, the assets are valued at the
most recent market prices. The reader is advised that
accountants have discretion of using other techniques for
valuation of assets but a discussion of these goes beyond
the intended scope of this text. All of the assets are
ultimately owned by either the stockholders or the creditors
(banks). The right side of the fundamental accounting equation
(liabilities and owner equity) depicts the relative amounts
owned by these two groups at the end of the fiscal period.

SALES SUMMARY

The marketing department of a firm develops the sales
report for each period. This sales summary indicates both
in units and dollars (based on the firm's selling price) the
actual and potential sales for the period. If insufficient
finished goods are available to satisfy the sales potential
then stockouts result. (For more detail on the implications
of stockouts see Chapters 3 and 4.) The share of the market
indicates the relative sales of the firm compared to the sales
total for the industry.

MATERIALS MANAGEMENT REPORT

The production department of the firm would maintain

records concerning the inventory and changes in inventory for leather, rubber and finished goods. The records for leather and rubber are based on square feet and for finished goods on units (i.e. pairs of finished shoes). The ending inventory for any period represents the beginning inventory for the next period. The waste factors are reported as of the *current period*.

LABOR AVAILABILITY AND UTILIZATION REPORT

This report would also be generated by the production managers. The first part of the report shows changes in effective capacity due to the influence of capital investment and depreciation (See Chapter 4 for details).

The second part of the report indicates the effect of downtime on scheduled labor during the *current period*.

ECONOMIC FORECASTS AND MARKET RESEARCH

The economic advisors of the firm are responsible for generating economic forecasts. The marketing department would generate the market research data. A more complete explanation of these reports is given in Chapter 2.

SUMMARY

This Appendix is designed to provide additional background on the statements and reports that are generated for the DECIDE firm. Its purpose is to assist the untrained user in understanding the sources and meaning of the reports commonly generated by a firm. Some of the most frequently encountered student misunderstandings and misconceptions are considered in this Appendix.

Appendix II:
A Discussion of Elasticities

The purpose of this Appendix is (i) to discuss briefly the concept of elasticity, and (ii) to illustrate the importance of certain elasticities in DECIDE managerial decision making.

ELASTICITY

DECIDE managers should be concerned with the impact on their major sales of changes in major decision variables such as price, promotion, and R & D.

A concept useful in dealing with the impact of changes is that of elasticity. In general an elasticity may be thought of as a ratio of relative changes in one quantity (or variable) to the relative changes in another, *ceteris paribus**. In other words, elasticities measure how responsive some dependent variable is to changes in a particular independent variable, while holding all other relevant variables or factors constant. The most commonly used elasticity in demand theory is that of price elasticity of demand. Price elasticity of demand, E_p, is defined as the percentage change in the quantity demanded of a particular good relative to a percentage change in the price of that good, all other factors held constant.

$E_p = \dfrac{\% \text{ Change in } Q_D}{\% \text{ Change in p}}$ where Q_D represents the quantity demanded and P is the price of the good.

---

* *Ceteris paribus* means all other things constant or equal.

The sign of the price elasticity of demand, as long as there is an inverse relationship between price of the good and the sales of the good, will always be negative; thus a price elasticity of -3 implies that as price increases (say by 1%) then sales will be expected to fall by about 3%, assuming all other relevant factors that influence sales are held constant. Prior to discussing the managerial implications of the elasticity of demand (price elasticity), other common elasticities are briefly described.

Other Elasticities

Any elasticity can be constructed by merely investigating the effect on a dependent variable of small changes in an independent variable, *ceteris paribus*.

The DECIDE manager might be interested in investigating the impact of R & D expenditures upon sales while keeping other influential variables constant. Thus, the R & D elasticity would be developed as follows:

$$E_{R \& D} = \frac{\% \text{ Change in } Q_D}{\% \text{ Change in R \& D}}$$

where R & D would represent the firm's expenditures in Research and Development

Likewise, the DECIDE manager might find it valuable to know the impact on sales potential of an additional dollar in promotion.

Thus, the promotion elasticity would be an important statistic.

$$E = \frac{\% \text{ Change in } Q_D}{\% \text{ Change in Prom.}}$$

where Prom. is promotion expenditure

Unfortunately, in practice accurate estimates on elasticities are difficult to determine.[1] The major reason stems from the fact that the assumption of all other things equal is difficult to maintain. In reality many other variables are changing at the same time that the dependent variable and the specified independent variable are changing.

Price Elasticity of Demand

One of the more important relationships derived from price elasticity of demand is the effect on sales and revenues of a change in price. Thus, price elasticity of demand, E_p, not only provides guidance in determining whether the team's price is too high or too low. Economists summarize relationships as follows:

When the price elasticity of demand is said to be unit elastic (i.e. $E_p = -1.$), then a percentage change in price is matched by an equal percentage change in sales. Thus, minor changes in price will *not* influence the total sales revenue received by the firm.

When the price elasticity of demand is elastic (i.e.

---

[1]To *approximate* the true elasticity one can use the following arc measure of elasticity:

$$E_X = \frac{\dfrac{Q_2 - Q_1}{(Q_2 + Q_1)/2}}{\dfrac{X_2 - X_1}{(X_2 + X_1)/2}}$$

where X is the independent variable of interest such as price, promotion, R & D etc. and Q is sales or quantity demanded.

$E_p < -1$, say -3) a percentage change in sales is exceeded by the percentage change in price. If the demand is elastic, a small decrease in price will increase sales (more than proportionately) and, thus, increase total revenues to the firm.

When the price elasticity of demand is inelastic (i.e. $E_q > -1.00$, say -.05), it follows that a decrease in price is not exceeded by changes in the sales volume. Thus, decreases in price would lower the total revenues of the firm.

To overcome the problem that all other variables must remain constant, a controlled experiment was performed where only one relevant variable was changed and its impact on sales was measured and put into the form of an elasticity. The impact of price and promotion and R & D were analyzed separately. A summary of the findings is presented.

DECIDE ELASTICITIES — CONTROLLED TEST

To illustrate the elasticities typically confronting firms in DECIDE, a controlled test was performed. The simulation consisted of six firms within the same DECIDE industry. Each team made the three marketing mix decisions - price, promotion, and R & D - for seven periods. To insure that all other things remained constant, the team varied only its price, promotion or R & D expenditures. Initially, all teams had a price of 25 dollars, spent 500,000 dollars on promotion and 300,000 dollars on research and development.

THE FINDINGS

The price elasticity of demand at the beginning of the experiment, period 1, was approximately -3. The experimental team which pursued modest increases in price *not matched* by R & D or promotion increases had an ending elasticity greater than -5. This elasticity suggests that such a strategy would cause a net decrease in sales revenue. This is not surprising since the firm did not increase promotion or R & D. For both R & D and promotion, the initial elasticities were approximately 1.85 for the experimental firm that held the other two variables constant. However, over time the experimental firm raising either R & D or promotion realized a decreasing elasticity. At the end of seven periods both elasticities were less than 1.0. This indicates that saturation might be occurring and less than proportional sales increases were being observed.

SUMMARY

DECIDE managers should be aware of the nature of the price elasticity of demand for their product. At the beginning of the game the price elasticity of demand is elastic and, thus, quite responsive to changes in price. However, a firm may differentiate its product by planned expenditures in both R & D and promotion. The simulation illustrates that saturation (diminishing returns) does set in for promotion and R & D. Thus, the DECIDE firm should establish a marketing mix plan early in the game.

DECIDE PRODUCTION WORKSHEET FOR TEAM _____ INDUSTRY _____ PERIOD _____

ESTIMATE FOR MAXIMUM PRODUCTION

RAW MATERIAL CONSTRAINTS AND ESTIMATES FOR WASTE AND DOWNTIME

LEATHER: (A) _____ = WASTE FACTOR % ÷ 100.
(BEGINNING INVENTORY IN SQ. FT.)

1. _____
   (1. × (A))

2. _____

3. _____

3L. _____ (3. ÷ 2.00: MAXIMUM PRODUCTION BASED
             UPON LEATHER CONSTRAINT)

RUBBER: (B) _____ = WASTE FACTOR % ÷ 100.
(BEGINNING INVENTORY IN SQ. FT.)

1. _____
   (1. × (B))

2. _____

3R. _____ (MAXIMUM PRODUCTION BASED UPON
             RUBBER CONSTRAINT)

LABOR CONSTRAINT

LABOR: (C) _____ = DOWNTIME % ÷ 100.
(CAPACITY IN LABOR HOURS WITH OVERTIME)

1. _____
   (1. × (C))

2. _____

3LA. _____ (MAXIMUM PRODUCTION BASED UPON
              THE LABOR CONSTRAINT)

CHOOSE THE SMALLEST OF 3R, 3L, and 3LA FOR MAXIMUM PRODUCTION _____ 1MP

ESTIMATE OF RAW MATERIALS USED AND ENDING INVENTORY FOR LEATHER AND RUBBER

LEATHER:

1. _____
   (BEGINNING INVENTORY IN SQ. FT.)

2. _____
   (MATERIAL USED: [1DP _____ ÷ [1.00 - (A) _____]] × 2.00)

3. _____
   (RAW MATERIAL PURCHASED IN SQ. FT.)

4. _____
   (ENDING INVENTORY IN SQ. FT.)

RUBBER:

1. _____
   (BEGINNING INVENTORY IN SQ. FT.)

2. _____
   (MATERIAL USED: [1DP _____ ÷ [1.00 - (B) _____]])

3. _____
   (RAW MATERIAL PURCHASED IN SQ. FT.)

4. _____
   (ENDING INVENTORY IN SQ. FT.)

DESIRED PRODUCTION _____ 1DP

ESTIMATE OF LABOR REQUIRED TO MEET DESIRED PRODUCTION (1DP)

1. _____
   (LABOR REQUIRED: [1DP _____ ÷ [1.00 - (c) _____]])

FROM PREVIOUS PERIOD'S LABOR AVAILABILITY AND UTILIZATION REPORT AND THE ESTIMATE OF LABOR REQUIRED:

TOTAL REGULAR TIME HOURS REQUIRED _____

TOTAL OVERTIME HOURS REQUIRED _____

ESTIMATED INCOME STATEMENT AND CASHFLOW BASED UPON SALES _____ 1$ AND A PRICE OF _____ 1P

DECIDE FINANCIAL WORKSHEET FOR TEAM _____   INDUSTRY _____   PERIOD _____

INCOME STATEMENT ESTIMATED:

1. TOTAL SALES REVENUE (1$ _____ x _____ 1P) = _____ 1.

COST OF GOODS PRODUCED:

a   BEGINNING INVENTORY OF FINISHED GOODS = _____
b + LABOR
  + OVERTIME PREMIUM
  + LEATHER USED
  + RUBBER USED
  = COST OF GOODS AVAILABLE

- ENDING INVENTORY OF FINISHED GOODS

2. = COST OF GOODS PRODUCED _____ 2.
3. = (1. - 2.) GROSS PROFIT (1. _____ - 2. _____) = _____ 3.

OPERATING EXPENSES: (ESTIMATES)

c Supervisory
d Maintenance
- Depreciation
e Interest Expense
f Ordering Cost for Leather
g Ordering Cost for Rubber
h Carrying Cost for Leather
i Carrying Cost for Rubber
j Carrying Cost for Finished Goods
k Carrying Cost for Rubber
l Carrying Cost for Finished Goods
  Promotion
  Research and Development
  Market Research
  Economic Research
  Misc. Operating Expenses

4. TOTAL OPERATING EXPENSES = _____ 4.

5. (3. - 4.) NET INCOME FROM SALES = _____ 5.

6. NET INCOME FROM MARKETABLE SECURITIES + _____ 6.

7. TOTAL TAXABLE INCOME (5. + 6.) = _____ 7.

8. INCOME TAXES (.48 x _____ 7.) - _____ 8.

9. NET INCOME AFTER TAXES (7. - 8.) = _____ 9.

CASH FLOW ESTIMATED:

CASH INFLOWS:

A. SALES REVENUE (1. _____) =
+C. SALE OF MARKETABLE SECURITIES
+C. INTEREST FROM MARKETABLE SECURITIES
+D. NET INCOME TAX CREDIT (if 7. is negative)
=E. TOTAL CASH INFLOW

CASH OUTFLOWS:

F. PURCHASE OF LEATHER
+G. PURCHASE OF RUBBER
+H. OPERATING EXPENSES REPRESENTING
    CASH OUTFLOWS:

a. _____	h. _____
b. _____	i. _____
c. _____	j. _____
d. _____	k. _____
e. _____	l. _____
f. _____	m. _____
g. _____	n. _____
	o. _____

    SUM OF CASH FLOW OPERATING EXPENSES
+I. PURCHASE OF MARKETABLE SECURITIES
+J. DIVIDENDS
+K. NET INCOME TAX EXPENSE (if 7. is positive)
+L. CAPITAL INVESTMENT
=M. TOTAL CASH OUTFLOW

NET CASH FLOW (E. _____ - M. _____) =

ESTIMATED CASH BALANCE

    PREVIOUS CASH BALANCE
+   NET CASH FLOW
=   ESTIMATED CASH BALANCE

DECISION SHEET

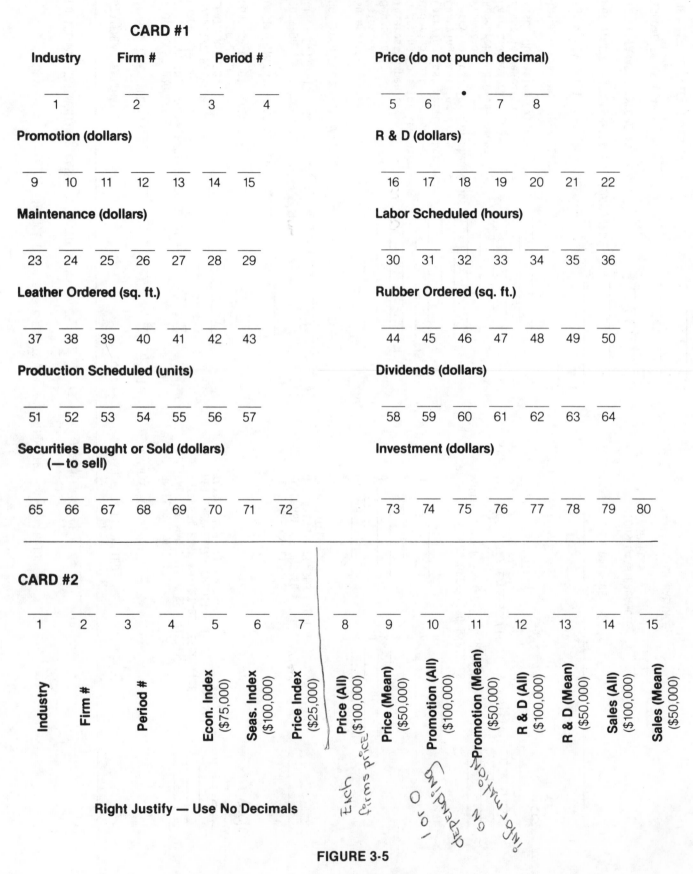

CARD #1

Industry	Firm #	Period #	
1	2	3	4

Price (do not punch decimal)

| 5 | 6 | • | 7 | 8 |

Promotion (dollars)

| 9 | 10 | 11 | 12 | 13 | 14 | 15 |

R & D (dollars)

| 16 | 17 | 18 | 19 | 20 | 21 | 22 |

Maintenance (dollars)

| 23 | 24 | 25 | 26 | 27 | 28 | 29 |

Labor Scheduled (hours)

| 30 | 31 | 32 | 33 | 34 | 35 | 36 |

Leather Ordered (sq. ft.)

| 37 | 38 | 39 | 40 | 41 | 42 | 43 |

Rubber Ordered (sq. ft.)

| 44 | 45 | 46 | 47 | 48 | 49 | 50 |

Production Scheduled (units)

| 51 | 52 | 53 | 54 | 55 | 56 | 57 |

Dividends (dollars)

| 58 | 59 | 60 | 61 | 62 | 63 | 64 |

Securities Bought or Sold (dollars)
(— to sell)

| 65 | 66 | 67 | 68 | 69 | 70 | 71 | 72 |

Investment (dollars)

| 73 | 74 | 75 | 76 | 77 | 78 | 79 | 80 |

CARD #2

1	2	3	4	5	6	7	8	9	10	11	12	13	14	15
Industry	Firm #	Period #	Econ. Index ($75,000)	Seas. Index ($100,000)	Price Index ($25,000)	Price (All) ($100,000)	Price (Mean) ($50,000)	Promotion (All) ($100,000)	Promotion (Mean) ($50,000)	R & D (All) ($100,000)	R & D (Mean) ($50,000)	Sales (All) ($100,000)	Sales (Mean) ($50,000)	

Right Justify — Use No Decimals

Each firms price

Information depending on 1 or 0

FIGURE 3-5

DECIDE PRODUCTION WORKSHEET FOR TEAM __2__ INDUSTRY __3__ PERIOD __01__

ESTIMATE FOR MAXIMUM PRODUCTION

RAW MATERIAL CONSTRAINTS AND ESTIMATES FOR WASTE AND DOWNTIME

LEATHER: (A) __.10__ = WASTE FACTOR % ÷ 100.   RUBBER: (B) __.10__ = WASTE FACTOR % ÷ 100.

1. __900,000__(BEGINNING INVENTORY IN SQ. FT.)   1. __1,500,000__(BEGINNING INVENTORY IN SQ. FT.)

−2. __90,000__(1. × (A))   −2. __50,000__(1. × (B))

= 3. __810,000__   3R. __450,000__(MAXIMUM PRODUCTION BASED UPON
                                                    RUBBER CONSTRAINT)

= 3L. __405,000__(3. ÷ 2.00: MAXIMUM PRODUCTION BASED
                    UPON LEATHER CONSTRAINT)

CHOOSE THE SMALLEST OF 3R, 3L, and 3LA FOR MAXIMUM PRODUCTION __405,000__ 1MP   DESIRED PRODUCTION __405,000__ 1DP

ESTIMATE OF RAW MATERIALS USED AND ENDING INVENTORY FOR LEATHER AND RUBBER

LEATHER: RUBBER:

1. __900,000__ (BEGINNING INVENTORY IN SQ. FT.)   1. __1,500,000__ (BEGINNING INVENTORY IN SQ. FT.)

−2. __900,000__(MATERIAL USED: [1DP __405,000__ ÷ [1.00 − (A) __.10__]] × 2.00)   −2. __450,000__(MATERIAL USED: [1DP __405,000__ ÷ [1.00 − (B) __.10__]])

+3. __900,000__ (RAW MATERIAL PURCHASED IN SQ. FT.)   +3. __450,000__(RAW MATERIAL PURCHASED IN SQ. FT.)

= 4. __1,000,000__ (ENDING INVENTORY IN SQ. FT.)   = 4. __500,000__(ENDING INVENTORY IN SQ. FT.)

ESTIMATE OF LABOR REQUIRED TO MEET DESIRED PRODUCTION (1DP)

1. __456,387__ (LABOR REQUIRED: [1DP __405,000__ ÷ [1.00 − (C) __.1124__]])

FROM PREVIOUS PERIOD'S LABOR AVAILABILITY AND UTILIZATION REPORT AND THE ESTIMATE OF LABOR REQUIRED:

TOTAL REGULAR TIME HOURS REQUIRED __400,000__

TOTAL OVERTIME HOURS REQUIRED __56,387__

LABOR CONSTRAINT

LABOR: (C) __.1124__ = DOWNTIME % ÷ 100.

1. __1,600,000__(CAPACITY IN LABOR HOURS WITH OVERTIME

−2. __67,440__(1. × (C))

= 3LA.__533,56__(MAXIMUM PRODUCTION BASED UPON
                    THE LABOR CONSTRAINT)

ESTIMATED INCOME STATEMENT AND CASHFLOW BASED UPON SALES __415,000__ 1S

AND A PRICE OF __27.00__ 1P

INCOME STATEMENT ESTIMATED:

1. TOTAL SALES REVENUE (1S __405,000__ x __27.00__ 1P) = 11,205,000.

   COST OF GOODS PRODUCED:
   a   BEGINNING INVENTORY OF FINISHED GOODS = __130,000__
   b + LABOR   __3,200,000__
      + OVERTIME PREMIUM   __675,444__
      + LEATHER USED   __1,58?,000__
      + RUBBER USED   __80,000__
      = COST OF GOODS AVAILABLE   __6,405,444__

   - ENDING INVENTORY OF FINISHED GOODS   0

2. = COST OF GOODS PRODUCED   __6,405,444__   2.
3. = (1. - 2.) GROSS PROFIT (1. 11,205,000 - 2. 6,405,444 = 4,799,000)3,556   3,556

OPERATING EXPENSES: (ESTIMATES)

   c   Supervisory   __650,000__
   d   Maintenance   __485,000__
   i   Depreciation
   e   Interest Expense
   f   Ordering Cost for Leather   __100,000__
   g   Ordering Cost for Rubber   __100,000__
   h   Carrying Cost for Leather   __135,000__
   i   Carrying Cost for Rubber   __100,000__
   j   Carrying Cost for Finished Goods   __135,000__
   k   Promotion   __750,000__
   l   Research and Development   __450,000__
   m   Market Research   __400,000__
   n   Economic Research   __300,000__
   o   Misc. Operating Expenses

4. TOTAL OPERATING EXPENSES   = 3,333,000.   4.

5. (3. - 4.) NET INCOME FROM SALES   = 1,476,556.   5.

6. NET INCOME FROM MARKETABLE SECURITIES + 78,000.   6.

7. TOTAL TAXABLE INCOME (5. + 6.)   = 1,484,356.   7.

8. INCOME TAXES (.48 x 1,484,356)   - 712,490.88   8.

9. NET INCOME AFTER TAXES (7. - 8.)   = 771,865.29   9.

CASH FLOW ESTIMATED:

CASH INFLOWS:

A. SALES REVENUE (1. 11,205,000) =   11,205,000
+B. SALE OF MARKETABLE SECURITIES
+C. INTEREST FROM MARKETABLE SECURITIES   78,000
+D. NET INCOME TAX CREDIT (if 7. is negative)   0
=E. TOTAL CASH INFLOW   11,283,000

CASH OUTFLOWS:

F. PURCHASE OF LEATHER   1,500,000
+G. PURCHASE OF RUBBER   9,000
+H. OPERATING EXPENSES REPRESENTING
    CASH OUTFLOWS:

    a. 3,200,000
    b. 675,444
    c. 650,000
    d. 100,000
    e.
    f. 100,000
    g. 100,000
    h. 135,000
    i. 100,000
    j. 135,000
    k. 750,000
    l. 450,000
    m. 400,000
    n. 300,000
    o.

SUM OF CASH FLOW OPERATING EXPENSES   6,773,444
+I. PURCHASE OF MARKETABLE SECURITIES
+J. DIVIDENDS   3,000,000
+K. NET INCOME TAX EXPENSE (if 7. is positive) 712,490.88
+L. CAPITAL INVESTMENT   3,000,000
=M. TOTAL CASH OUTFLOW   10,535,934.88

NET CASH FLOW

    (E. 11,283,000 - M. 10,535,934.88 676,865.12)

ESTIMATED CASH BALANCE

    + PREVIOUS CASH BALANCE   3,000,000
    - NET CASH FLOW   676,865.12

    = ESTIMATED CASH BALANCE   3,676,865.12

DECISION SHEET

CARD #1

Industry	Firm #	Period #		Price (do not punch decimal)

‾1‾   ‾2‾   ‾3‾ ‾4‾   ‾5‾ ‾6‾ • ‾7‾ ‾8‾

Promotion (dollars)   **R & D (dollars)**

‾9‾ ‾10‾ ‾11‾ ‾12‾ ‾13‾ ‾14‾ ‾15‾   ‾16‾ ‾17‾ ‾18‾ ‾19‾ ‾20‾ ‾21‾ ‾22‾

Maintenance (dollars)   **Labor Scheduled (hours)**

‾23‾ ‾24‾ ‾25‾ ‾26‾ ‾27‾ ‾28‾ ‾29‾   ‾30‾ ‾31‾ ‾32‾ ‾33‾ ‾34‾ ‾35‾ ‾36‾

Leather Ordered (sq. ft.)   **Rubber Ordered (sq. ft.)**

‾37‾ ‾38‾ ‾39‾ ‾40‾ ‾41‾ ‾42‾ ‾43‾   ‾44‾ ‾45‾ ‾46‾ ‾47‾ ‾48‾ ‾49‾ ‾50‾

Production Scheduled (units)   **Dividends (dollars)**

‾51‾ ‾52‾ ‾53‾ ‾54‾ ‾55‾ ‾56‾ ‾57‾   ‾58‾ ‾59‾ ‾60‾ ‾61‾ ‾62‾ ‾63‾ ‾64‾

Securities Bought or Sold (dollars)   **Investment (dollars)**
(— to sell)

‾65‾ ‾66‾ ‾67‾ ‾68‾ ‾69‾ ‾70‾ ‾71‾ ‾72‾   ‾73‾ ‾74‾ ‾75‾ ‾76‾ ‾77‾ ‾78‾ ‾79‾ ‾80‾

CARD #2

1	2	3	4	5	6	7	8	9	10	11	12	13	14	15
Industry	Firm #	Period #	Econ. Index ($75,000)	Seas. Index ($100,000)	Price Index ($25,000)	Price (All) ($100,000)	Price (Mean) ($50,000)	Promotion (All) ($100,000)	Promotion (Mean) ($50,000)	R & D (All) ($100,000)	R & D (Mean) ($50,000)	Sales (All) ($100,000)	Sales (Mean) ($50,000)	

Right Justify — Use No Decimals

FIGURE 3-5

DECIDE PRODUCTION WORKSHEET FOR TEAM _2_ INDUSTRY _3_ PERIOD _2_

ESTIMATE FOR MAXIMUM PRODUCTION

RAW MATERIAL CONSTRAINTS AND ESTIMATES FOR WASTE AND DOWNTIME

LEATHER: (A) _10_ = WASTE FACTOR % ÷ 100.   RUBBER: (B) _10_ = WASTE FACTOR % ÷ 100.

1. _1,000,000_ (BEGINNING INVENTORY IN SQ. FT.)   1. _1,550,000_ (BEGINNING INVENTORY IN SQ. FT.)

−2. _.10_ (1. × (A))   −2. _55,000_ (1. × (B)):

= 3. _900,000_   =

= 3L. _450,000_ (3. ÷ 2.00: MAXIMUM PRODUCTION   3R. _495,000_ (MAXIMUM PRODUCTION BASED UPON
         UPON LEATHER CONSTRAINT)   RUBBER CONSTRAINT)

CHOOSE THE SMALLEST OF 3R, 3L, and 3LA FOR MAXIMUM PRODUCTION _450,000_ 1MP   DESIRED PRODUCTION _450,000_ 1DP

ESTIMATE OF RAW MATERIALS USED AND ENDING INVENTORY FOR LEATHER AND RUBBER

LEATHER: RUBBER:

1. _1,000,000_ (BEGINNING INVENTORY IN SQ. FT.)   1. _1,550,000_ (BEGINNING INVENTORY IN SQ. FT.)

−2. _1,000,000_ (MATERIAL USED: [1DP _450,000_ ÷ [1.00 − (A) _.10_]] × 2.00)   −2. _500,000_ (MATERIAL USED: [1DP _450,000_ ÷ [1.00 − (B) _.10_]])

+3. _1,200,000_ (RAW MATERIAL PURCHASED IN SQ. FT.)   +3. _0_ (RAW MATERIAL PURCHASED IN SQ. FT.)

= 4. _1,200,000_ (ENDING INVENTORY IN SQ. FT.)   = 4. _1,050,000_ (ENDING INVENTORY IN SQ. FT.)

ESTIMATE OF LABOR REQUIRED TO MEET DESIRED PRODUCTION (1DP)
                                                   _450,000_
1. _501,616.32_ (LABOR REQUIRED: [1DP _450,000_ ÷ [1.00 − (C) _.1032_]])

LABOR CONSTRAINT
                                                     LABOR: (C) _.1032_ = DOWNTIME % ÷ 100.

1. _1,043,875_ (CAPACITY IN LABOR HOURS WITH OVERTIME)

−2. _6,3,319_ (1. × (C))

= 3LA. _551,556.19_ (MAXIMUM PRODUCTION BASED UPON THE LABOR CONSTRAINT)

FROM PREVIOUS PERIOD'S LABOR AVAILABILITY AND UTILIZATION REPORT AND THE ESTIMATE OF LABOR REQUIRED:

TOTAL REGULAR TIME HOURS REQUIRED _409,683_

TOTAL OVERTIME HOURS REQUIRED _93,033.32_

DECIDE FINANCIAL WORKSHEET FOR TEAM _2_   INDUSTRY _3_   PERIOD _2_

ESTIMATED INCOME STATEMENT AND CASHFLOW BASED UPON SALES _450,000_ 1S   AND A PRICE OF _27.00_ 1P

INCOME STATEMENT ESTIMATED:

1. TOTAL SALES REVENUE (1S _450,000_ x _27.00_ 1P) = _12,150,000_

COST OF GOODS PRODUCED:
BEGINNING INVENTORY OF FINISHED GOODS =

a	+ LABOR	3,276,994
b	+ OVERTIME PREMIUM	104,390.84
	+ LEATHER USED	1,950,000
	+ RUBBER USED	1,300,000
	= COST OF GOODS AVAILABLE	7,531,063.84

- ENDING INVENTORY OF FINISHED GOODS _____ 6

2. = COST OF GOODS PRODUCED _____ 7,531,063.84
3. = (1. - 2.) GROSS PROFIT (_12,150,000_ - 2. _7,531,063.84_) = 3. _4,618,936.16_

OPERATING EXPENSES: (ESTIMATES)

c	Supervisory	750,000
d	Maintenance	500,000
-	Depreciation	
e	Interest Expense	100,000
f	Ordering Cost for Leather	
g	Ordering Cost for Rubber	
h	Carrying Cost for Leather	135,000
i	Carrying Cost for Rubber	
j	Carrying Cost for Finished Goods	13,000
k	Promotion	500,000
l	Research and Development	575,000
m	Market Research	400,000
n	Economic Research	
o	Misc. Operating Expenses	0

4. TOTAL OPERATING EXPENSES _____ 3,473,000

5. (3. - 4.) NET INCOME FROM SALES = _1,145,936.16_

6. NET INCOME FROM MARKETABLE SECURITIES + _73,000_

7. TOTAL TAXABLE INCOME (5. + 6.) = _1,159,736.16_

8. INCOME TAXES (.48 x _____ 7.) - _553,793.36_

9. NET INCOME AFTER TAXES (7. - 8.) = _599,943.80_

CASH FLOW ESTIMATED:

CASH INFLOWS:

A. SALES REVENUE (1. _12,150,000_) = _12,150,000_
+B. SALE OF MARKETABLE SECURITIES
+C. INTEREST FROM MARKETABLE SECURITIES
+D. NET INCOME TAX CREDIT (if 7. is negative)
=E. TOTAL CASH INFLOW

CASH OUTFLOWS:

F. PURCHASE OF LEATHER _____ 1,950,000
+G. PURCHASE OF RUBBER _____ 1,300,000
+H. OPERATING EXPENSES REPRESENTING CASH OUTFLOWS:

a.	3,276,994
b.	104,390.84
c.	
d.	75,000
e.	
f.	100,000
g.	
h.	135,000
i.	100,000
j.	13,000
k.	500,000
l.	575,000
m.	
n.	400,000
o.	

SUM OF CASH FLOW OPERATING EXPENSES _____ 7,354,063.84
+I. PURCHASE OF MARKETABLE SECURITIES
+J. DIVIDENDS _____ 60,000
+K. NET INCOME TAX EXPENSE (if 7. is positive) _____ 553,793.36
+L. CAPITAL INVESTMENT _____ 300,000
=M. TOTAL CASH OUTFLOW _____ 11,967,857.20

NET CASH FLOW   (E. _____ - M. _____) =

ESTIMATED CASH BALANCE

PREVIOUS CASH BALANCE _____
+ NET CASH FLOW _____

= ESTIMATED CASH BALANCE _____

DECISION SHEET

CARD #1

Industry   Firm #   Period #   Price (do not punch decimal)

___	___	___	___		___	___	•	___	___
1	2	3	4		5	6		7	8

Promotion (dollars)

___	___	___	___	___	___	___
9	10	11	12	13	14	15

R & D (dollars)

___	___	___	___	___	___	___
16	17	18	19	20	21	22

Maintenance (dollars)

___	___	___	___	___	___	___
23	24	25	26	27	28	29

Labor Scheduled (hours)

___	___	___	___	___	___	___
30	31	32	33	34	35	36

Leather Ordered (sq. ft.)

___	___	___	___	___	___	___
37	38	39	40	41	42	43

Rubber Ordered (sq. ft.)

___	___	___	___	___	___	___
44	45	46	47	48	49	50

Production Scheduled (units)

___	___	___	___	___	___	___
51	52	53	54	55	56	57

Dividends (dollars)

___	___	___	___	___	___	___
58	59	60	61	62	63	64

Securities Bought or Sold (dollars)
    (— to sell)

___	___	___	___	___	___	___	___
65	66	67	68	69	70	71	72

Investment (dollars)

___	___	___	___	___	___	___	___
73	74	75	76	77	78	79	80

CARD #2

1	2	3	4	5	6	7	8	9	10	11	12	13	14	15
Industry	Firm #	Period #	Econ. Index ($75,000)	Seas. Index ($100,000)	Price Index ($25,000)	Price (All) ($100,000)	Price (Mean) ($50,000)	Promotion (All) ($100,000)	Promotion (Mean) ($50,000)	R & D (All) ($100,000)	R & D (Mean) ($50,000)	Sales (All) ($100,000)	Sales (Mean) ($50,000)

Right Justify — Use No Decimals

FIGURE 3-5

DECIDE PRODUCTION WORKSHEET FOR TEAM 2 INDUSTRY 3 PERIOD 03

ESTIMATE FOR MAXIMUM PRODUCTION

RAW MATERIAL CONSTRAINTS AND ESTIMATES FOR WASTE AND DOWNTIME

LEATHER: (A) .10 = WASTE FACTOR % ÷ 100. RUBBER: (B) .10 = WASTE FACTOR % ÷ 100. LABOR: (C) .063 = DOWNTIME % ÷ 100.

1. 1303767 (BEGINNING INVENTORY IN SQ. FT.)   1. 951883 (BEGINNING INVENTORY IN SQ. FT.)   1. 913390 (CAPACITY IN LABOR HOURS WITH OVERTIME

-2. 1303767 (1. × (A))   -2. 951883 (3. × (B))   -2. 65303 (1.57 × (C))

= 3. 1173390.3   = 3R. _____ (MAXIMUM PRODUCTION BASED UPON   = 3LA. 54 (MAXIMUM PRODUCTION BASED UPON
                                                     RUBBER CONSTRAINT)   THE LABOR CONSTRAINT)
= 3L. 586695 (3.55 ÷ 2.00: MAXIMUM PRODUCTION   586994.7   548187 /.013
   BASED UPON LEATHER CONSTRAINT)

CHOOSE THE SMALLEST OF 3R, 3L, and 3LA FOR MAXIMUM PRODUCTION 548187 1MP   DESIRED PRODUCTION 548187 1DP

ESTIMATE OF RAW MATERIALS USED AND ENDING INVENTORY FOR LEATHER AND RUBBER

LEATHER: RUBBER:

1. 1303767 (BEGINNING INVENTORY IN SQ. FT.)   1. 651883 (BEGINNING INVENTORY IN SQ. FT.)

-2. 1303767 (MATERIAL USED: [1DP ___ ÷ [1.00 - (A) .16]] × 2.00)   -2. 600097 (MATERIAL USED: [1DP ___ ÷ [1.00 - (B) .10]])
   586994.7   586994.7

+3. 750000 (RAW MATERIAL PURCHASED IN SQ. FT.)   +3. 793786 (RAW MATERIAL PURCHASED IN SQ. FT.)

= 4. _____ (ENDING INVENTORY IN SQ. FT.)   = 4. _____ (ENDING INVENTORY IN SQ. FT.)

ESTIMATE OF LABOR REQUIRED TO MEET DESIRED PRODUCTION (1DP)

1. _____ (LABOR REQUIRED: [1DP ___ ÷ [1.00 - (C) ___]])

FROM PREVIOUS PERIOD'S LABOR AVAILABILITY AND UTILIZATION REPORT AND THE ESTIMATE OF LABOR REQUIRED:

TOTAL REGULAR TIME HOURS REQUIRED _____

TOTAL OVERTIME HOURS REQUIRED _____

DECIDE FINANCIAL WORKSHEET FOR TEAM 6   INDUSTRY 3   PERIOD 03

ESTIMATED INCOME STATEMENT AND CASHFLOW BASED UPON SALES 548187 1s   AND A PRICE OF 28.00 1P

INCOME STATEMENT ESTIMATED:

1. TOTAL SALES REVENUE (1S 548187 x 28.00 1P) = 15349236

COST OF GOODS PRODUCED:
BEGINNING INVENTORY OF FINISHED GOODS = 0

a	+ LABOR	3336844.30
b	+ OVERTIME PREMIUM	3503037.10
	+ LEATHER USED	1803805.80
	+ RUBBER USED	1348557.88
	= COST OF GOODS AVAILABLE	8945865.1

    - ENDING INVENTORY OF FINISHED GOODS   0

2. = COST OF GOODS PRODUCED   8945865.12.
3. = (1. - 2.) GROSS PROFIT (1.15349236 - 2.8945865) = 6403371.88 3.

OPERATING EXPENSES: (ESTIMATES)

c	Supervisory	900000
d	Maintenance	4393.75
-	Depreciation	
-	Interest Expense	
e	Ordering Cost for Leather	103000
f	Ordering Cost for Rubber	103000
g	Carrying Cost for Leather	153000
h	Carrying Cost for Rubber	112000
j	Carrying Cost for Finished Goods	
k	Promotion	800000
l	Research and Development	
m	Market Research	400000
n	Economic Research	400000
o	Misc. Operating Expenses	

4. TOTAL OPERATING EXPENSES = 3498575 4.

5. (3. - 4.) NET INCOME FROM SALES = 2904796 + 5.

6. NET INCOME FROM MARKETABLE SECURITIES = 37800 6.

7. TOTAL TAXABLE INCOME (5. + 6.) = 2833596 - 7.

8. INCOME TAXES (.48 x ____ 7.) = 1350406 8.

9. NET INCOME AFTER TAXES (7. - 8.) = 1473050 9.

CASH FLOW ESTIMATED:

CASH INFLOWS:

A.	SALES REVENUE (1. 15349236) =	15349236
+B.	SALE OF MARKETABLE SECURITIES	—
+C.	INTEREST FROM MARKETABLE SECURITIES	37800
+D.	NET INCOME TAX CREDIT (if 7. is negative)	—
=E.	TOTAL CASH INFLOW	15388036

CASH OUTFLOWS:

F.	PURCHASE OF LEATHER	3395000
+G.	PURCHASE OF RUBBER	1500301
+H.	OPERATING EXPENSES REPRESENTING	
	CASH OUTFLOWS:	

h.	153000
i.	112000
j.	—
k.	800000
l.	—
m.	400000
n.	400000
o.	0

SUM OF CASH FLOW OPERATING EXPENSES

a.	3336844.30
b.	3503037.10
c.	900000
d.	—
e.	103000
f.	103000
g.	0

+I.	PURCHASE OF MARKETABLE SECURITIES	
+J.	DIVIDENDS	12833367.14
+K.	NET INCOME TAX EXPENSE (if 7. is positive)	147395
+L.	CAPITAL INVESTMENT	1350406
=M.	TOTAL CASH OUTFLOW	1500000 15390913.40

NET CASH FLOW

(E. _____ - M. _____) = _____

ESTIMATED CASH BALANCE

    PREVIOUS CASH BALANCE   -56304
+ NET CASH FLOW   453,576

= ESTIMATED CASH BALANCE

DECISION SHEET

CARD #1

Industry	Firm #	Period #
___	___	___ ___
1	2	3 4

Price (do not punch decimal)

___ ___ • ___ ___
5 6 7 8

Promotion (dollars)

___ ___ ___ ___ ___ ___ ___
9 10 11 12 13 14 15

R & D (dollars)

___ ___ ___ ___ ___ ___ ___
16 17 18 19 20 21 22

Maintenance (dollars)

___ ___ ___ ___ ___ ___ ___
23 24 25 26 27 28 29

Labor Scheduled (hours)

___ ___ ___ ___ ___ ___ ___
30 31 32 33 34 35 36

Leather Ordered (sq. ft.)

___ ___ ___ ___ ___ ___ ___
37 38 39 40 41 42 43

Rubber Ordered (sq. ft.)

___ ___ ___ ___ ___ ___ ___
44 45 46 47 48 49 50

Production Scheduled (units)

___ ___ ___ ___ ___ ___ ___
51 52 53 54 55 56 57

Dividends (dollars)

___ ___ ___ ___ ___ ___ ___
58 59 60 61 62 63 64

Securities Bought or Sold (dollars)
(— to sell)

___ ___ ___ ___ ___ ___ ___ ___
65 66 67 68 69 70 71 72

Investment (dollars)

___ ___ ___ ___ ___ ___ ___ ___
73 74 75 76 77 78 79 80

CARD #2

1	2	3	4	5	6	7	8	9	10	11	12	13	14	15
Industry	Firm #	Period #	Econ. Index ($75,000)	Seas. Index ($100,000)	Price Index ($25,000)	Price (All) ($100,000)	Price (Mean) ($50,000)	Promotion (All) ($100,000)	Promotion (Mean) ($50,000)	R & D (All) ($100,000)	R & D (Mean) ($50,000)	Sales (All) ($100,000)	Sales (Mean) ($50,000)	

Right Justify — Use No Decimals

FIGURE 3-5

DECIDE PRODUCTION WORKSHEET FOR TEAM 2 INDUSTRY 3 PERIOD 7

ESTIMATE FOR MAXIMUM PRODUCTION

RAW MATERIAL CONSTRAINTS AND ESTIMATES FOR WASTE AND DOWNTIME

LEATHER: (A) .10 = WASTE FACTOR % ÷ 100.   RUBBER: (B) .10 = WASTE FACTOR % ÷ 100.

1. 1458714 (BEGINNING INVENTORY IN SQ. FT.)   1. 1527113 (BEGINNING INVENTORY IN SQ. FT.)

-2. 1458714 (1. × (A))   -2. 1527113 (1. × (B));

= 1339843.6   =

3. 1339843.6   3R. 6774441 (MAXIMUM PRODUCTION BASED UPON RUBBER CONSTRAINT)

3L. _____ (3. ÷ 2.00: MAXIMUM PRODUCTION BASED UPON LEATHER CONSTRAINT)

CHOOSE THE SMALLEST OF 3R, 3L, and 3LA FOR MAXIMUM PRODUCTION _____ 1MP   DESIRED PRODUCTION _____ 1DP

LABOR CONSTRAINT

LABOR: (C) 698 = DOWNTIME % ÷ 100.

1. _____ (CAPACITY IN LABOR HOURS WITH OVERTIME

-2. _____ (1. × (C))

= 3LA. _____ (MAXIMUM PRODUCTION BASED UPON THE LABOR CONSTRAINT)

ESTIMATE OF RAW MATERIALS USED AND ENDING INVENTORY FOR LEATHER AND RUBBER

LEATHER:

1. _____ (BEGINNING INVENTORY IN SQ. FT.)

-2. _____ (MATERIAL USED: [1DP _____ ÷ [1.00 - (A) _____]] × 2.00)

+3. 1,000,000 (RAW MATERIAL PURCHASED IN SQ. FT.)

=4. 900,000 (ENDING INVENTORY IN SQ. FT.)

RUBBER:

1. 1744536 (BEGINNING INVENTORY IN SQ. FT.)

-2. _____ (MATERIAL USED: [1DP _____ ÷ [1.00 - (B) _____]])

+3. 500 (RAW MATERIAL PURCHASED IN SQ. FT.)

=4. 500 (ENDING INVENTORY IN SQ. FT.)

ESTIMATE OF LABOR REQUIRED TO MEET DESIRED PRODUCTION (1DP)

1. 73019 (LABOR REQUIRED: [1DP _____ ÷ [1.00 - (C) 302]])

FROM PREVIOUS PERIOD'S LABOR AVAILABILITY AND UTILIZATION REPORT AND THE ESTIMATE OF LABOR REQUIRED:

TOTAL REGULAR TIME HOURS REQUIRED 517930

TOTAL OVERTIME HOURS REQUIRED 260965

DECIDE FINANCIAL WORKSHEET FOR TEAM _____ INDUSTRY _____ PERIOD _____

ESTIMATED INCOME STATEMENT AND CASHFLOW BASED UPON SALES _____ 1S AND A PRICE OF _____ 1P

INCOME STATEMENT ESTIMATED:

1. TOTAL SALES REVENUE (1S _649930_ × _30.00_ 1P) = 30097600 1.   30,097,400

COST OF GOODS PRODUCED:
BEGINNING INVENTORY OF FINISHED GOODS = _25597_

a + LABOR _4479915_
b + OVERTIME PREMIUM _930806_
   + LEATHER USED
   + RUBBER USED
   = COST OF GOODS AVAILABLE _1186542_

  − ENDING INVENTORY OF FINISHED GOODS

2. = COST OF GOODS PRODUCED   2.
3. = (1. − 2.) GROSS PROFIT (1. _____ − 2. _____) = _____   3.

OPERATING EXPENSES: (ESTIMATES)

c   Supervisory
d   Maintenance INCREASED DOWNTIME 1,100,600
−   Depreciation
e   Interest Expense
f   Ordering Cost for Leather
g   Ordering Cost for Rubber
h   Carrying Cost for Leather
i   Carrying Cost for Rubber
j   Carrying Cost for Finished Goods
k   Promotion
l   Research and Development
m   Market Research
n   Economic Research
o   Misc. Operating Expenses

4. TOTAL OPERATING EXPENSES   4.

5. (3. − 4.) NET INCOME FROM SALES   =   5.

6. NET INCOME FROM MARKETABLE SECURITIES   +   6.

7. TOTAL TAXABLE INCOME (5. + 6.)   =   7.

8. INCOME TAXES (.48 × _____ 7.)   −   8.

9. NET INCOME AFTER TAXES (7. − 8.)   =   9.

CASH FLOW ESTIMATED:

CASH INFLOWS:

A. SALES REVENUE (1. _____) =   30,097,400
+B. SALE OF MARKETABLE SECURITIES
+C. INTEREST FROM MARKETABLE SECURITIES
+D. NET INCOME TAX CREDIT (if 7. is negative)
=E. TOTAL CASH INFLOW

CASH OUTFLOWS:

F. PURCHASE OF LEATHER
+G. PURCHASE OF RUBBER
+H. OPERATING EXPENSES REPRESENTING
    CASH OUTFLOWS:

    a. _____   h. _____
    b. _____   i. _____
    c. _____   j. _____
    d. _____   k. _____
    e. _____   l. _____
    f. _____   m. _____
    g. _____   n. _____
                       o. _____

    SUM OF CASH FLOW OPERATING EXPENSES
+I. PURCHASE OF MARKETABLE SECURITIES
+J. DIVIDENDS
+K. NET INCOME TAX EXPENSE (if 7. is positive)
+L. CAPITAL INVESTMENT
=M. TOTAL CASH OUTFLOW

NET CASH FLOW

    (E. _____ − M. _____) =

ESTIMATED CASH BALANCE

    PREVIOUS CASH BALANCE
+   NET CASH FLOW

=   ESTIMATED CASH BALANCE

DECISION SHEET

CARD #1

Industry   Firm #   Period #

$\overline{}$ $\overline{}$ $\overline{}$ $\overline{}$
1   2   3   4

Price (do not punch decimal)

$\overline{}$ $\overline{}$ • $\overline{}$ $\overline{}$
5   6   7   8

Promotion (dollars)

9   10   11   12   13   14   15

R & D (dollars)

16   17   18   19   20   21   22

Maintenance (dollars)

23   24   25   26   27   28   29

Labor Scheduled (hours)

30   31   32   33   34   35   36

Leather Ordered (sq. ft.)

37   38   39   40   41   42   43

Rubber Ordered (sq. ft.)

44   45   46   47   48   49   50

Production Scheduled (units)

51   52   53   54   55   56   57

Dividends (dollars)

58   59   60   61   62   63   64

Securities Bought or Sold (dollars)
(— to sell)

65   66   67   68   69   70   71   72

Investment (dollars)

73   74   75   76   77   78   79   80

CARD #2

1	2	3	4	5	6	7	8	9	10	11	12	13	14	15
Industry	Firm #	Period #	Econ. Index ($75,000)	Seas. Index ($100,000)	Price Index ($25,000)	Price (All) ($100,000)	Price (Mean) ($50,000)	Promotion (All) ($100,000)	Promotion (Mean) ($50,000)	R & D (All) ($100,000)	R & D (Mean) ($50,000)	Sales (All) ($100,000)	Sales (Mean) ($50,000)	

Right Justify — Use No Decimals

FIGURE 3-5

DECIDE PRODUCTION WORKSHEET FOR TEAM _____ INDUSTRY _____ PERIOD _____

ESTIMATE FOR MAXIMUM PRODUCTION

RAW MATERIAL CONSTRAINTS AND ESTIMATES FOR WASTE AND DOWNTIME

LEATHER: (A) _____ = WASTE FACTOR % ÷ 100.   RUBBER: (B) _____ = WASTE FACTOR % ÷ 100.   LABOR CONSTRAINT

LABOR: (C) _____ = DOWNTIME % ÷ 100.

1. _____ (BEGINNING INVENTORY IN SQ. FT.)

-2. _____ (1. × (A))

= 3. _____

3L. _____ (3. ÷ 2.00: MAXIMUM PRODUCTION BASED UPON LEATHER CONSTRAINT)

1. _____ (BEGINNING INVENTORY IN SQ. FT.)

-2. _____ (1. × (B))

= 3R. _____ (MAXIMUM PRODUCTION BASED UPON RUBBER CONSTRAINT)

1. _____ (CAPACITY IN LABOR HOURS WITH OVERTIME

-2. _____ (1. × (C))

= 3LA. _____ (MAXIMUM PRODUCTION BASED UPON THE LABOR CONSTRAINT)

CHOOSE THE SMALLEST OF 3R, 3L, and 3LA FOR MAXIMUM PRODUCTION _____ 1MP   DESIRED PRODUCTION _____ 1DP

ESTIMATE OF RAW MATERIALS USED AND ENDING INVENTORY FOR LEATHER AND RUBBER

LEATHER:

1. _____ (BEGINNING INVENTORY IN SQ. FT.)

-2. _____ (MATERIAL USED: [1DP _____ ÷ [1.00 - (A) _____]] × 2.00)

+3. _____ (RAW MATERIAL PURCHASED IN SQ. FT.)

= 4. _____ (ENDING INVENTORY IN SQ. FT.)

RUBBER:

1. _____ (BEGINNING INVENTORY IN SQ. FT.)

-2. _____ (MATERIAL USED: [1DP _____ ÷ [1.00 - (B) _____]])

+3. _____ (RAW MATERIAL PURCHASED IN SQ. FT.)

= 4. _____ (ENDING INVENTORY IN SQ. FT.)

ESTIMATE OF LABOR REQUIRED TO MEET DESIRED PRODUCTION (1DP)

1. _____ (LABOR REQUIRED: [1DP _____ ÷ [1.00 - (C) _____]])

FROM PREVIOUS PERIOD'S LABOR AVAILABILITY AND UTILIZATION REPORT AND THE ESTIMATE OF LABOR REQUIRED:

TOTAL REGULAR TIME HOURS REQUIRED _____

TOTAL OVERTIME HOURS REQUIRED _____

DECIDE FINANCIAL WORKSHEET FOR TEAM _____ INDUSTRY _____ PERIOD _____

ESTIMATED INCOME STATEMENT AND CASHFLOW BASED UPON SALES _____ 1$ AND A PRICE OF _____ 1P

INCOME STATEMENT ESTIMATED: CASH FLOW ESTIMATED:

1. TOTAL SALES REVENUE (1S _____ x _____ 1P) = _____ 1.   CASH INFLOWS:

   COST OF GOODS PRODUCED: A. SALES REVENUE (1. _____) =
   BEGINNING INVENTORY OF FINISHED GOODS = _____   +B. SALE OF MARKETABLE SECURITIES
a + LABOR   _____   +C. INTEREST FROM MARKETABLE SECURITIES
b + OVERTIME PREMIUM   _____   +D. NET INCOME TAX CREDIT (if 7. is negative)
   + LEATHER USED   _____   =E. TOTAL CASH INFLOW
   + RUBBER USED   _____
   = COST OF GOODS AVAILABLE   _____   CASH OUTFLOWS:

   - ENDING INVENTORY OF FINISHED GOODS   F. PURCHASE OF LEATHER   _____
                                        _____   +G. PURCHASE OF RUBBER   _____
2. = COST OF GOODS PRODUCED   _____ 2.   +H. OPERATING EXPENSES REPRESENTING
3. = (1. - 2.) GROSS PROFIT (1. _____ - 2. _____) = _____ 3.   CASH OUTFLOWS:

OPERATING EXPENSES: (ESTIMATES)   a. _____
                                                                                      b. _____
c   Supervisory   _____   c. _____
d   Maintenance   _____   d. _____
-    Depreciation   _____   e. _____
-    Interest Expense   _____   f. _____
e   Ordering Cost for Leather   _____   g. _____
f   Ordering Cost for Rubber   _____   h. _____
g   Carrying Cost for Leather   _____   i. _____
h   Carrying Cost for Rubber   _____   j. _____
i   Carrying Cost for Finished Goods _____   k. _____
j   Promotion   _____   l. _____
k   Research and Development   _____   m. _____
l   Market Research   _____   n. _____
m   Economic Research   _____   o. _____
n   Misc. Operating Expenses   _____
o   SUM OF CASH FLOW OPERATING EXPENSES
                                                                                 +I. PURCHASE OF MARKETABLE SECURITIES
4.   TOTAL OPERATING EXPENSES   _____ 4.   +J. DIVIDENDS
                                                                                 +K. NET INCOME TAX EXPENSE (if 7. is positive)
5.   (3. - 4.) NET INCOME FROM SALES = _____ 5.   +L. CAPITAL INVESTMENT
                                                                                 =M. TOTAL CASH OUTFLOW
6.   NET INCOME FROM MARKETABLE SECURITIES + _____ 6.
                                                                                 NET CASH FLOW
7.   TOTAL TAXABLE INCOME (5. + 6.) = _____ 7.
                                                                                    (E. _____ - M. _____) = _____
8.   INCOME TAXES (.48 x _____ 7.) - _____ 8.
                                                                                 ESTIMATED CASH BALANCE
9.   NET INCOME AFTER TAXES (7. - 8.) = _____ 9.
                                                                                     PREVIOUS CASH BALANCE   _____
                                                                                 +   NET CASH FLOW   _____

                                                                                 =   ESTIMATED CASH BALANCE   _____

DECISION SHEET

CARD #1

Industry	Firm #	Period #			Price (do not punch decimal)				

    1   2   3   4   5   6   •   7   8

Promotion (dollars)   **R & D (dollars)**

9   10   11   12   13   14   15   16   17   18   19   20   21   22

Maintenance (dollars)   **Labor Scheduled (hours)**

23   24   25   26   27   28   29   30   31   32   33   34   35   36

Leather Ordered (sq. ft.)   **Rubber Ordered (sq. ft.)**

37   38   39   40   41   42   43   44   45   46   47   48   49   50

Production Scheduled (units)   **Dividends (dollars)**

51   52   53   54   55   56   57   58   59   60   61   62   63   64

Securities Bought or Sold (dollars)   **Investment (dollars)**
    (— to sell)

65   66   67   68   69   70   71   72   73   74   75   76   77   78   79   80

CARD #2

1   2   3   4   5   6   7   8   9   10   11   12   13   14   15

Col	Label
1	Industry
2	Firm #
3	Period #
4	Econ. Index ($75,000)
5	Seas. Index ($100,000)
6	Price Index ($25,000)
7	Price (All) ($100,000)
8	Price (Mean) ($50,000)
9	Promotion (All) ($100,000)
10	Promotion (Mean) ($50,000)
11	R & D (All) ($100,000)
12	R & D (Mean) ($50,000)
13	Sales (All) ($100,000)
14	Sales (Mean) ($50,000)

Right Justify — Use No Decimals

FIGURE 3-5

DECIDE PRODUCTION WORKSHEET FOR TEAM _____ INDUSTRY _____ PERIOD _____

ESTIMATE FOR MAXIMUM PRODUCTION
RAW MATERIAL CONSTRAINTS AND ESTIMATES FOR WASTE AND DOWNTIME

LEATHER: (A) _____ = WASTE FACTOR % ÷ 100.   RUBBER: (B) _____ = WASTE FACTOR % ÷ 100.

1. _____ (BEGINNING INVENTORY IN SQ. FT.)   1. _____ (BEGINNING INVENTORY IN SQ. FT.)

‾ 2. _____ (1. × (A))   ‾ 2. _____ (1. × (B));

= 3. _____   = 3R. _____ (MAXIMUM PRODUCTION BASED UPON
                                                              RUBBER CONSTRAINT)
= 3L. _____ (3. ÷ 2.00: MAXIMUM PRODUCTION BASED
              UPON LEATHER CONSTRAINT)

LABOR CONSTRAINT

LABOR: (C) _____ = DOWNTIME % ÷ 100.

1. _____ (CAPACITY IN LABOR HOURS WITH OVERTIME

‾ 2. _____ (1. × (C))

= 3LA. _____ (MAXIMUM PRODUCTION BASED UPON
               THE LABOR CONSTRAINT)

CHOOSE THE SMALLEST OF 3R, 3L, and 3LA FOR MAXIMUM PRODUCTION _____ 1MP   DESIRED PRODUCTION _____ 1DP

ESTIMATE OF RAW MATERIALS USED AND ENDING INVENTORY FOR LEATHER AND RUBBER

LEATHER: RUBBER:

1. _____ (BEGINNING INVENTORY IN SQ. FT.)   1. _____ (BEGINNING INVENTORY IN SQ. FT.)

‾ 2. _____ (MATERIAL USED: [1DP _____ ÷ [1.00 - (A) _____]] × 2.00)   ‾ 2. _____ (MATERIAL USED: [1DP _____ ÷ [1.00 - (B) _____]])

+ 3. _____ (RAW MATERIAL PURCHASED IN SQ. FT.)   + 3. _____ (RAW MATERIAL PURCHASED IN SQ. FT.)

= 4. _____ (ENDING INVENTORY IN SQ. FT.)   = 4. _____ (ENDING INVENTORY IN SQ. FT.)

ESTIMATE OF LABOR REQUIRED TO MEET DESIRED PRODUCTION (1DP)

1. _____ (LABOR REQUIRED: [1DP _____ ÷ [1.00 - (C) _____]])

FROM PREVIOUS PERIOD'S LABOR AVAILABILITY AND UTILIZATION REPORT AND THE ESTIMATE OF LABOR REQUIRED:

TOTAL REGULAR TIME HOURS REQUIRED _____

TOTAL OVERTIME HOURS REQUIRED _____

DECIDE FINANCIAL WORKSHEET FOR TEAM _____ INDUSTRY _____ PERIOD _____

ESTIMATED INCOME STATEMENT AND CASHFLOW BASED UPON SALES _____ 1S AND A PRICE OF _____ 1P

INCOME STATEMENT ESTIMATED:

1. TOTAL SALES REVENUE (1S _____ x _____ 1P) = _____ 1.

COST OF GOODS PRODUCED:
BEGINNING INVENTORY OF FINISHED GOODS = _____

a + LABOR _____
b + OVERTIME PREMIUM _____
   + LEATHER USED _____
   + RUBBER USED _____
   = COST OF GOODS AVAILABLE _____

   - ENDING INVENTORY OF FINISHED GOODS _____

2. = COST OF GOODS PRODUCED _____ 2.
3. = (1. - 2.) GROSS PROFIT (1. _____ - 2. _____) = _____ 3.

OPERATING EXPENSES: (ESTIMATES)

c Supervisory _____
d Maintenance _____
- Depreciation _____
e Interest Expense _____
f Ordering Cost for Leather _____
g Ordering Cost for Rubber _____
h Carrying Cost for Leather _____
i Carrying Cost for Rubber _____
j Carrying Cost for Finished Goods _____
k Promotion _____
l Research and Development _____
m Market Research _____
n Economic Research _____
o Misc. Operating Expenses _____

4. TOTAL OPERATING EXPENSES _____ 4.

5. (3. - 4.) NET INCOME FROM SALES _____ = 5.

6. NET INCOME FROM MARKETABLE SECURITIES _____ + 6.

7. TOTAL TAXABLE INCOME (5. + 6.) _____ = 7.

8. INCOME TAXES (.48 x _____ 7.) _____ - 8.

9. NET INCOME AFTER TAXES (7. - 8.) _____ = 9.

CASH FLOW ESTIMATED:

CASH INFLOWS:

A. SALES REVENUE (1. _____) = _____
+B. SALE OF MARKETABLE SECURITIES _____
+C. INTEREST FROM MARKETABLE SECURITIES _____
+D. NET INCOME TAX CREDIT (if 7. is negative) _____
=E. TOTAL CASH INFLOW _____

CASH OUTFLOWS:

F. PURCHASE OF LEATHER _____
+G. PURCHASE OF RUBBER _____
+H. OPERATING EXPENSES REPRESENTING
    CASH OUTFLOWS:

    a. _____
    b. _____
    c. _____
    d. _____
    e. _____
    f. _____
    g. _____

    h. _____
    i. _____
    j. _____
    k. _____
    l. _____
    m. _____
    n. _____
    o. _____

SUM OF CASH FLOW OPERATING EXPENSES _____
+I. PURCHASE OF MARKETABLE SECURITIES _____
+J. DIVIDENDS _____
+K. NET INCOME TAX EXPENSE (if 7. is positive) _____
+L. CAPITAL INVESTMENT _____
=M. TOTAL CASH OUTFLOW _____

NET CASH FLOW
(E. _____ - M. _____) = _____

ESTIMATED CASH BALANCE

    PREVIOUS CASH BALANCE _____
  + NET CASH FLOW _____

  = ESTIMATED CASH BALANCE _____

DECISION SHEET

CARD #1

Industry	Firm #	Period #
‾1	‾2	‾3 ‾4

Price (do not punch decimal)

‾5 ‾6 • ‾7 ‾8

Promotion (dollars)

‾9 ‾10 ‾11 ‾12 ‾13 ‾14 ‾15

R & D (dollars)

‾16 ‾17 ‾18 ‾19 ‾20 ‾21 ‾22

Maintenance (dollars)

‾23 ‾24 ‾25 ‾26 ‾27 ‾28 ‾29

Labor Scheduled (hours)

‾30 ‾31 ‾32 ‾33 ‾34 ‾35 ‾36

Leather Ordered (sq. ft.)

‾37 ‾38 ‾39 ‾40 ‾41 ‾42 ‾43

Rubber Ordered (sq. ft.)

‾44 ‾45 ‾46 ‾47 ‾48 ‾49 ‾50

Production Scheduled (units)

‾51 ‾52 ‾53 ‾54 ‾55 ‾56 ‾57

Dividends (dollars)

‾58 ‾59 ‾60 ‾61 ‾62 ‾63 ‾64

Securities Bought or Sold (dollars)
(— to sell)

‾65 ‾66 ‾67 ‾68 ‾69 ‾70 ‾71 ‾72

Investment (dollars)

‾73 ‾74 ‾75 ‾76 ‾77 ‾78 ‾79 ‾80

CARD #2

1	2	3	4	5	6	7	8	9	10	11	12	13	14	15
Industry	Firm #	Period #	Econ. Index ($75,000)	Seas. Index ($100,000)	Price Index ($25,000)	Price (All) ($100,000)	Price (Mean) ($50,000)	Promotion (All) ($100,000)	Promotion (Mean) ($50,000)	R & D (All) ($100,000)	R & D (Mean) ($50,000)	Sales (All) ($100,000)	Sales (Mean) ($50,000)	

Right Justify — Use No Decimals

FIGURE 3-5

DECIDE PRODUCTION WORKSHEET FOR TEAM _____ INDUSTRY _____ PERIOD _____

ESTIMATE FOR MAXIMUM PRODUCTION

RAW MATERIAL CONSTRAINTS AND ESTIMATES FOR WASTE AND DOWNTIME

LEATHER: (A) _____ = WASTE FACTOR % ÷ 100.   RUBBER: (B) _____ = WASTE FACTOR % ÷ 100.

1. _____ (BEGINNING INVENTORY IN SQ. FT.)   1. _____ (BEGINNING INVENTORY IN SQ. FT.)

- 2. _____ (1. x (A))   - 2. _____ (1. x (B));

=

3. _____ (MAXIMUM PRODUCTION BASED   3R. _____ (MAXIMUM PRODUCTION BASED UPON
   UPON LEATHER CONSTRAINT)   RUBBER CONSTRAINT)

= 3L. _____ (3. ÷ 2.00: MAXIMUM PRODUCTION BASED
   UPON LEATHER CONSTRAINT)

LABOR CONSTRAINT

LABOR: (C) _____ = DOWNTIME % ÷ 100.

1. _____ (CAPACITY IN LABOR HOURS WITH OVERTIME

- 2. _____ (1. x (C))

= 3LA. _____ (MAXIMUM PRODUCTION BASED UPON
   THE LABOR CONSTRAINT)

CHOOSE THE SMALLEST OF 3R, 3L, and 3LA FOR MAXIMUM PRODUCTION _____ 1MP   DESIRED PRODUCTION _____ 1DP

ESTIMATE OF RAW MATERIALS USED AND ENDING INVENTORY FOR LEATHER AND RUBBER

LEATHER: RUBBER:

1. _____ (BEGINNING INVENTORY IN SQ. FT.)   1. _____ (BEGINNING INVENTORY IN SQ. FT.)

- 2. _____ (MATERIAL USED: [1DP _____ ÷ [1.00 - (A) _____]] x 2.00)   - 2. _____ (MATERIAL USED: [1DP _____ ÷ [1.00 - (B) _____]])

+ 3. _____ (RAW MATERIAL PURCHASED IN SQ. FT.)   + 3. _____ (RAW MATERIAL PURCHASED IN SQ. FT.)

= 4. _____ (ENDING INVENTORY IN SQ. FT.)   = 4. _____ (ENDING INVENTORY IN SQ. FT.)

ESTIMATE OF LABOR REQUIRED TO MEET DESIRED PRODUCTION (1DP)

1. _____ (LABOR REQUIRED: [1DP _____ ÷ [1.00 - (C) _____]])

FROM PREVIOUS PERIOD'S LABOR AVAILABILITY AND UTILIZATION REPORT AND THE ESTIMATE OF LABOR REQUIRED:

TOTAL REGULAR TIME HOURS REQUIRED _____

TOTAL OVERTIME HOURS REQUIRED _____

DECIDE FINANCIAL WORKSHEET FOR TEAM _____ INDUSTRY _____ PERIOD _____

AND A PRICE OF _____ 1P _____

ESTIMATED INCOME STATEMENT AND CASHFLOW BASED UPON SALES _____ 1S

INCOME STATEMENT ESTIMATED:

1. TOTAL SALES REVENUE (1S _____ x _____ 1P) = _____ 1. _____

COST OF GOODS PRODUCED:
BEGINNING INVENTORY OF FINISHED GOODS = _____
a + LABOR _____
b + OVERTIME PREMIUM _____
+ LEATHER USED _____
+ RUBBER USED _____
= COST OF GOODS AVAILABLE _____

- ENDING INVENTORY OF FINISHED GOODS _____

2. = COST OF GOODS PRODUCED _____ 2. _____
3. = (1. - 2.) GROSS PROFIT (1. _____ - 2. _____) = _____ 3. _____

OPERATING EXPENSES: (ESTIMATES)

c   Supervisory _____
d   Maintenance _____
-    Depreciation _____
e   Interest Expense _____
f   Ordering Cost for Leather _____
g   Ordering Cost for Rubber _____
h   Carrying Cost for Leather _____
i   Carrying Cost for Rubber _____
j   Carrying Cost for Finished Goods _____
k   Promotion _____
l   Research and Development _____
m   Market Research _____
n   Economic Research _____
o   Misc. Operating Expenses _____

4.   TOTAL OPERATING EXPENSES _____ 4. _____

5.   (3. - 4.) NET INCOME FROM SALES = _____ 5. _____

6.   NET INCOME FROM MARKETABLE SECURITIES + _____ 6. _____

7.   TOTAL TAXABLE INCOME (5. + 6.) = _____ 7. _____

8.   INCOME TAXES (.48 x _____ 7.) - _____ 8. _____

9.   NET INCOME AFTER TAXES (7. - 8.) = _____ 9. _____

CASH FLOW ESTIMATED:

CASH INFLOWS:

A.   SALES REVENUE (1. _____) = _____
+B. SALE OF MARKETABLE SECURITIES _____
+C. INTEREST FROM MARKETABLE SECURITIES _____
+D. NET INCOME TAX CREDIT (if 7. is negative) _____
=E. TOTAL CASH INFLOW _____

CASH OUTFLOWS:

F.   PURCHASE OF LEATHER _____
+G. PURCHASE OF RUBBER _____
+H. OPERATING EXPENSES REPRESENTING
     CASH OUTFLOWS:
                                    h. _____
                                    i. _____
                                    j. _____
                                    k. _____
                                    l. _____
                                    m. _____
                                    n. _____
                                    o. _____

     SUM OF CASH FLOW OPERATING EXPENSES _____
+I. PURCHASE OF MARKETABLE SECURITIES _____
+J. DIVIDENDS _____
+K. NET INCOME TAX EXPENSE (if 7. is positive) _____
+L. CAPITAL INVESTMENT _____
=M. TOTAL CASH OUTFLOW _____

NET CASH FLOW

     (E. _____ - M. _____) = _____

ESTIMATED CASH BALANCE

     PREVIOUS CASH BALANCE _____
+   NET CASH FLOW _____

=   ESTIMATED CASH BALANCE _____

DECISION SHEET

CARD #1

Industry	Firm #	Period #		Price (do not punch decimal)

1	2	3	4		5	6	•	7	8

Promotion (dollars)

9	10	11	12	13	14	15

R & D (dollars)

16	17	18	19	20	21	22

Maintenance (dollars)

23	24	25	26	27	28	29

Labor Scheduled (hours)

30	31	32	33	34	35	36

Leather Ordered (sq. ft.)

37	38	39	40	41	42	43

Rubber Ordered (sq. ft.)

44	45	46	47	48	49	50

Production Scheduled (units)

51	52	53	54	55	56	57

Dividends (dollars)

58	59	60	61	62	63	64

Securities Bought or Sold (dollars)
(— to sell)

65	66	67	68	69	70	71	72

Investment (dollars)

73	74	75	76	77	78	79	80

CARD #2

1	2	3	4	5	6	7	8	9	10	11	12	13	14	15
Industry	Firm #	Period #	Econ. Index ($75,000)	Seas. Index ($100,000)	Price Index ($25,000)	Price (All) ($100,000)	Price (Mean) ($50,000)	Promotion (All) ($100,000)	Promotion (Mean) ($50,000)	R & D (All) ($100,000)	R & D (Mean) ($50,000)	Sales (All) ($100,000)	Sales (Mean) ($50,000)	

Right Justify — Use No Decimals

FIGURE 3-5

DECIDE PRODUCTION WORKSHEET FOR TEAM _____ INDUSTRY _____ PERIOD _____

ESTIMATE FOR MAXIMUM PRODUCTION

RAW MATERIAL CONSTRAINTS AND ESTIMATES FOR WASTE AND DOWNTIME

LEATHER: (A) _____ = WASTE FACTOR % ÷ 100.   RUBBER: (B) _____ = WASTE FACTOR % ÷ 100.

1. _____ (BEGINNING INVENTORY IN SQ. FT.)   1. _____ (BEGINNING INVENTORY IN SQ. FT.)

-2. _____ (1. × (A))   -2. _____ (1. × (B));

= 3. _____   = _____

= 3L. _____ (3. ÷ 2.00: MAXIMUM PRODUCTION BASED   3R. _____ (MAXIMUM PRODUCTION BASED UPON
             UPON LEATHER CONSTRAINT)   RUBBER CONSTRAINT)

LABOR CONSTRAINT

LABOR: (C) _____ = DOWNTIME % ÷ 100.

1. _____ (CAPACITY IN LABOR HOURS WITH OVERTIME

-2. _____ (1. × (C))

= 3LA. _____ (MAXIMUM PRODUCTION BASED UPON
              THE LABOR CONSTRAINT)

CHOOSE THE SMALLEST OF 3R, 3L, and 3LA FOR MAXIMUM PRODUCTION _____ 1MP   DESIRED PRODUCTION _____ 1DP

ESTIMATE OF RAW MATERIALS USED AND ENDING INVENTORY FOR LEATHER AND RUBBER

LEATHER: RUBBER:

1. _____ (BEGINNING INVENTORY IN SQ. FT.)   1. _____ (BEGINNING INVENTORY IN SQ. FT.)

-2. _____ (MATERIAL USED: [1DP _____ ÷ [1.00 - (A) _____]] × 2.00)   -2. _____ (MATERIAL USED: [1DP _____ ÷ [1.00 - (B) _____]])

+3. _____ (RAW MATERIAL PURCHASED IN SQ. FT.)   +3. _____ (RAW MATERIAL PURCHASED IN SQ. FT.)

=4. _____ (ENDING INVENTORY IN SQ. FT.)   =4. _____ (ENDING INVENTORY IN SQ. FT.)

ESTIMATE OF LABOR REQUIRED TO MEET DESIRED PRODUCTION (1DP)

1. _____ (LABOR REQUIRED: [1DP _____ ÷ [1.00 - (C) _____]])

FROM PREVIOUS PERIOD'S LABOR AVAILABILITY AND UTILIZATION REPORT AND THE ESTIMATE OF LABOR REQUIRED:

TOTAL REGULAR TIME HOURS REQUIRED _____

TOTAL OVERTIME HOURS REQUIRED _____

DECIDE FINANCIAL WORKSHEET FOR TEAM _____ INDUSTRY _____ PERIOD _____

ESTIMATED INCOME STATEMENT AND CASHFLOW BASED UPON SALES _____ 1S AND A PRICE OF _____ 1P

INCOME STATEMENT ESTIMATED:

1. TOTAL SALES REVENUE (1S _____ x _____ 1P) = _____ 1.

   COST OF GOODS PRODUCED:
   BEGINNING INVENTORY OF FINISHED GOODS = _____
   a + LABOR _____
   b + OVERTIME PREMIUM _____
      + LEATHER USED _____
      + RUBBER USED _____
      = COST OF GOODS AVAILABLE _____

   - ENDING INVENTORY OF FINISHED GOODS _____

2. = COST OF GOODS PRODUCED _____ 2.
3. = (1. - 2.) GROSS PROFIT (1. _____ - 2. _____) = _____ 3.

OPERATING EXPENSES: (ESTIMATES)

   c Supervisory _____
   d Maintenance _____
   - Depreciation _____
   e Interest Expense _____
   f Ordering Cost for Leather _____
   g Ordering Cost for Rubber _____
   h Carrying Cost for Leather _____
   i Carrying Cost for Rubber _____
   j Carrying Cost for Finished Goods _____
   k Promotion _____
   l Research and Development _____
   m Market Research _____
   n Economic Research _____
   o Misc. Operating Expenses _____

4. TOTAL OPERATING EXPENSES _____ 4.

5. (3. - 4.) NET INCOME FROM SALES _____ = 5.

6. NET INCOME FROM MARKETABLE SECURITIES _____ + 6.

7. TOTAL TAXABLE INCOME (5. + 6.) _____ = 7.

8. INCOME TAXES (.48 x _____ 7.) _____ - 8.

9. NET INCOME AFTER TAXES (7. - 8.) _____ = 9.

CASH FLOW ESTIMATED:

CASH INFLOWS:

   A. SALES REVENUE (1. _____) = _____
   +B. SALE OF MARKETABLE SECURITIES _____
   +C. INTEREST FROM MARKETABLE SECURITIES _____
   +D. NET INCOME TAX CREDIT (if 7. is negative) _____
   =E. TOTAL CASH INFLOW _____

CASH OUTFLOWS:

   F. PURCHASE OF LEATHER _____
   +G. PURCHASE OF RUBBER _____
   +H. OPERATING EXPENSES REPRESENTING
       CASH OUTFLOWS:
       a. _____   h. _____
       b. _____   i. _____
       c. _____   j. _____
       d. _____   k. _____
       e. _____   l. _____
       f. _____   m. _____
       g. _____   n. _____
                    o. _____

   SUM OF CASH FLOW OPERATING EXPENSES _____
   +I. PURCHASE OF MARKETABLE SECURITIES _____
   +J. DIVIDENDS _____
   +K. NET INCOME TAX EXPENSE (if 7. is positive) _____
   +L. CAPITAL INVESTMENT _____
   =M. TOTAL CASH OUTFLOW _____

   NET CASH FLOW
       (E. _____ - M. _____) = _____

   ESTIMATED CASH BALANCE

       PREVIOUS CASH BALANCE _____
   +   NET CASH FLOW _____

   =   ESTIMATED CASH BALANCE _____

DECISION SHEET

CARD #1

Industry	Firm #	Period #
__1__	__2__	__3__ __4__

Price (do not punch decimal)

__5__ __6__ • __7__ __8__

Promotion (dollars)

__9__ __10__ __11__ __12__ __13__ __14__ __15__

R & D (dollars)

__16__ __17__ __18__ __19__ __20__ __21__ __22__

Maintenance (dollars)

__23__ __24__ __25__ __26__ __27__ __28__ __29__

Labor Scheduled (hours)

__30__ __31__ __32__ __33__ __34__ __35__ __36__

Leather Ordered (sq. ft.)

__37__ __38__ __39__ __40__ __41__ __42__ __43__

Rubber Ordered (sq. ft.)

__44__ __45__ __46__ __47__ __48__ __49__ __50__

Production Scheduled (units)

__51__ __52__ __53__ __54__ __55__ __56__ __57__

Dividends (dollars)

__58__ __59__ __60__ __61__ __62__ __63__ __64__

Securities Bought or Sold (dollars)
(— to sell)

__65__ __66__ __67__ __68__ __69__ __70__ __71__ __72__

Investment (dollars)

__73__ __74__ __75__ __76__ __77__ __78__ __79__ __80__

CARD #2

1	2	3	4	5	6	7	8	9	10	11	12	13	14	15
Industry	Firm #	Period #	Econ. Index ($75,000)	Seas. Index ($100,000)	Price Index ($25,000)	Price (All) ($100,000)	Price (Mean) ($50,000)	Promotion (All) ($100,000)	Promotion (Mean) ($50,000)	R & D (All) ($100,000)	R & D (Mean) ($50,000)	Sales (All) ($100,000)	Sales (Mean) ($50,000)	

Right Justify — Use No Decimals

FIGURE 3-5

DECIDE PRODUCTION WORKSHEET FOR TEAM _____ INDUSTRY _____ PERIOD _____

ESTIMATE FOR MAXIMUM PRODUCTION

RAW MATERIAL CONSTRAINTS AND ESTIMATES FOR WASTE AND DOWNTIME

LEATHER: (A) _____ = WASTE FACTOR % ÷ 100. RUBBER: (B) _____ = WASTE FACTOR % ÷ 100.

1. _____ (BEGINNING INVENTORY IN SQ. FT.) 1. _____ (BEGINNING INVENTORY IN SQ. FT.)

-2. _____ (1. × (A)) -2. _____ (1. × (B)).

= 3. _____ = 3R. _____ (MAXIMUM PRODUCTION BASED UPON RUBBER CONSTRAINT)

= 3L. _____ (3. ÷ 2.00: MAXIMUM PRODUCTION BASED UPON LEATHER CONSTRAINT)

LABOR CONSTRAINT

LABOR: (C) _____ = DOWNTIME % ÷ 100.

1. _____ (CAPACITY IN LABOR HOURS WITH OVERTIME)

-2. _____ (1. × (C))

= 3LA. _____ (MAXIMUM PRODUCTION BASED UPON THE LABOR CONSTRAINT)

CHOOSE THE SMALLEST OF 3R, 3L, and 3LA FOR MAXIMUM PRODUCTION _____ 1MP DESIRED PRODUCTION _____ 1DP

ESTIMATE OF RAW MATERIALS USED AND ENDING INVENTORY FOR LEATHER AND RUBBER

LEATHER:

1. _____ (BEGINNING INVENTORY IN SQ. FT.)

-2. _____ (MATERIAL USED: [1DP _____ ÷ [1.00 - (A) _____]] × 2.00)

+3. _____ (RAW MATERIAL PURCHASED IN SQ. FT.)

= 4. _____ (ENDING INVENTORY IN SQ. FT.)

RUBBER:

1. _____ (BEGINNING INVENTORY IN SQ. FT.)

-2. _____ (MATERIAL USED: [1DP _____ ÷ [1.00 - (B) _____]])

+3. _____ (RAW MATERIAL PURCHASED IN SQ. FT.)

= 4. _____ (ENDING INVENTORY IN SQ. FT.)

ESTIMATE OF LABOR REQUIRED TO MEET DESIRED PRODUCTION (1DP)

1. _____ (LABOR REQUIRED: [1DP _____ ÷ [1.00 - (C) _____]])

FROM PREVIOUS PERIOD'S LABOR AVAILABILITY AND UTILIZATION REPORT AND THE ESTIMATE OF LABOR REQUIRED:

TOTAL REGULAR TIME HOURS REQUIRED _____

TOTAL OVERTIME HOURS REQUIRED _____

DECIDE FINANCIAL WORKSHEET FOR TEAM _____ INDUSTRY _____ PERIOD _____

ESTIMATED INCOME STATEMENT AND CASHFLOW BASED UPON SALES _____ 1S AND A PRICE OF _____ 1P

INCOME STATEMENT ESTIMATED:

CASH FLOW ESTIMATED:

1. TOTAL SALES REVENUE (1S _____ x _____ 1P) = _____ 1.

CASH INFLOWS:

COST OF GOODS PRODUCED:
BEGINNING INVENTORY OF FINISHED GOODS = _____

a + LABOR _____
b + OVERTIME PREMIUM _____
+ LEATHER USED _____
+ RUBBER USED _____
= COST OF GOODS AVAILABLE _____

- ENDING INVENTORY OF FINISHED GOODS _____

2. = COST OF GOODS PRODUCED _____ 2.
3. = (1. - 2.) GROSS PROFIT (1. _____ - 2. _____) = _____ 3.

OPERATING EXPENSES: (ESTIMATES)

c   Supervisory _____
d   Maintenance _____
-    Depreciation _____
e   Interest Expense _____
f   Ordering Cost for Leather _____
g   Ordering Cost for Rubber _____
h   Carrying Cost for Leather _____
i   Carrying Cost for Rubber _____
j   Carrying Cost for Finished Goods _____
k   Promotion _____
l   Research and Development _____
m   Market Research _____
n   Economic Research _____
o   Misc. Operating Expenses _____

4.   TOTAL OPERATING EXPENSES _____ 4.

5.   (3. - 4.) NET INCOME FROM SALES _____ = _____ 5.

6.   NET INCOME FROM MARKETABLE SECURITIES _____ + _____ 6.

7.   TOTAL TAXABLE INCOME (5. + 6.) _____ = _____ 7.

8.   INCOME TAXES (.48 x _____ 7.) _____ - _____ 8.

9.   NET INCOME AFTER TAXES (7. - 8.) _____ = _____ 9.

CASH INFLOWS:

A.   SALES REVENUE (1. _____) = _____
+B. SALE OF MARKETABLE SECURITIES _____
+C. INTEREST FROM MARKETABLE SECURITIES _____
+D. NET INCOME TAX CREDIT (if 7. is negative) _____
=E. TOTAL CASH INFLOW _____

CASH OUTFLOWS:

F.   PURCHASE OF LEATHER _____
+G. PURCHASE OF RUBBER _____
+H. OPERATING EXPENSES REPRESENTING
     CASH OUTFLOWS:

     a. _____
     b. _____
     c. _____
     d. _____
     e. _____
     f. _____
     g. _____

     h. _____
     i. _____
     j. _____
     k. _____
     l. _____
     m. _____
     n. _____
     o. _____

     SUM OF CASH FLOW OPERATING EXPENSES _____
+I. PURCHASE OF MARKETABLE SECURITIES _____
+J. DIVIDENDS _____
+K. NET INCOME TAX EXPENSE (if 7. is positive) _____
+L. CAPITAL INVESTMENT _____
=M. TOTAL CASH OUTFLOW _____

NET CASH FLOW

     (E. _____ - M. _____) = _____

ESTIMATED CASH BALANCE

     PREVIOUS CASH BALANCE _____
+   NET CASH FLOW _____

=   ESTIMATED CASH BALANCE _____

DECISION SHEET

CARD #1

Industry	Firm #	Period #
3	2	0 1
1	2	3 4

Price (do not punch decimal)

2	7	.	0	0
5	6		7	8

Promotion (dollars)

_	7	5	0	0	0	0
9	10	11	12	13	14	15

R & D (dollars)

_	4	5	0	0	0	0
16	17	18	19	20	21	22

Maintenance (dollars)

_	6	5	0	0	0	0
23	24	25	26	27	28	29

Labor Scheduled (hours)

_	4	5	6	3	8	7
30	31	32	33	34	35	36

Leather Ordered (sq. ft.)

1	0	0	0	0	0	0
37	38	39	40	41	42	43

Rubber Ordered (sq. ft.)

_	5	0	0	0	0	0
44	45	46	47	48	49	50

Production Scheduled (units)

_	4	0	5	0	0	0
51	52	53	54	55	56	57

Dividends (dollars)

_	_	5	0	0	0	0
58	59	60	61	62	63	64

Securities Bought or Sold (dollars)
(— to sell)

_	2	0	0	0	0	0	0
65	66	67	68	69	70	71	72

Investment (dollars)

_	1	0	0	0	0	0	0
73	74	75	76	77	78	79	80

CARD #2

3	2	0	1	1	1	1	1	0	1	0	1	0	1	0
1	2	3	4	5	6	7	8	9	10	11	12	13	14	15

| Industry | Firm # | Period # | Econ. Index ($75,000) | Seas. Index ($100,000) | Price Index ($25,000) | Price (All) ($100,000) | Price (Mean) ($50,000) | Promotion (All) ($100,000) | Promotion (Mean) ($50,000) | R & D (All) ($100,000) | R & D (Mean) ($50,000) | Sales (All) ($100,000) | Sales (Mean) ($50,000) |

Right Justify — Use No Decimals

FIGURE 3-5